THE ULTIMATE GUIDE TO WEB DEVELOPMENT FRAMEWORKS

Master the Latest Web Technologies for Building Responsive Sites

THOMPSON CARTER

TABLE OF CONTENTS

Introduction

The Ultimate Guide to Web Development Frameworks

Web development has evolved significantly over the past few decades, and the tools and frameworks we use to build web applications have become increasingly powerful, flexible, and efficient. Whether you're a beginner eager to learn the fundamentals or an experienced developer looking to stay ahead of the curve, this book is your comprehensive guide to mastering the latest web development frameworks and technologies.

In *The Ultimate Guide to Web Development Frameworks*, we will take you on an in-depth journey through the landscape of modern web development, from understanding the basics to exploring the most advanced frameworks and tools that are shaping the future of web applications.

The Evolution of Web Development

The web development landscape has gone through significant transformations. Early websites were built using simple HTML and CSS, with limited interactivity. As the internet evolved, so did the demands of users and developers alike. Web applications grew in complexity, necessitating better tools to handle user interfaces, server-side logic, databases, and more.

Today, we have a diverse set of technologies that cater to different needs and use cases. Web frameworks have emerged to provide structure, streamline development, and offer reusable solutions to common problems. These frameworks are crucial in modern web development, helping developers build scalable, maintainable, and high-performance applications quickly and efficiently.

Why Frameworks Matter

Frameworks provide the foundation upon which web developers build applications. They offer a structured approach to development, streamline the coding process, and help maintain consistency across projects. Frameworks eliminate much of the repetitive coding work, allowing developers to focus on building unique features and solving complex problems.

A well-chosen framework can dramatically reduce development time, enhance code maintainability, and improve the overall user experience. In today's fast-paced development environment, using a framework not only boosts productivity but also ensures that applications are built with best practices in mind.

What You Will Learn

This book will explore the essential frameworks that define modern web development. We'll start by introducing you to the **fundamentals of web development**, including front-end and back-end development, responsive design, and the core technologies like HTML, CSS, and JavaScript.

Then, we'll dive into the various frameworks, covering both **front-end** and **back-end** solutions:

- **Front-End Frameworks**: We will explore popular JavaScript libraries and frameworks like **React**, **Angular**, and **Vue.js**, each offering unique features and solutions for building dynamic user interfaces. You'll learn how these frameworks help manage state, handle component-based architecture, and provide seamless user experiences.

- **Back-End Frameworks**: We will also delve into **Node.js**, **Express**, **Django**, **Ruby on Rails**, and others, showing how they handle server-side logic, database management, and API development. You'll gain practical knowledge of how these frameworks integrate with databases, manage user authentication, and deploy web applications.

- **Cross-Platform Solutions**: Learn how frameworks like **React Native** and **Electron** enable the development of mobile apps and desktop apps using web technologies, empowering developers to create cross-platform applications efficiently.

Additionally, we'll cover emerging trends such as **JAMstack** (JavaScript, APIs, and Markup), **WebAssembly**, **Serverless**

architectures, and the role of **Progressive Web Apps (PWAs)** in modern web development.

Real-World Examples

The core strength of this book lies in its **real-world examples**. Throughout the chapters, you will not only understand the theory behind each framework but also apply that knowledge to build actual projects. From creating a simple **React-based landing page** to deploying a **full-stack Node.js application**, the hands-on approach will help solidify your understanding and improve your problem-solving skills.

Each example is designed to build on your knowledge progressively, starting from basic concepts and moving toward more advanced techniques. By the end of the book, you'll be equipped with the skills necessary to confidently use the latest frameworks to build scalable and responsive web applications.

Why This Book?

Whether you're new to web development or an experienced developer, this book will provide you with the tools and knowledge you need to succeed. Web development frameworks can be overwhelming due to the sheer number of options available, but this book will help you navigate the ecosystem by focusing on the most important and widely used technologies.

What sets this book apart is its emphasis on practical, real-world application. You'll learn not only the theory behind web development frameworks but also how to apply that knowledge in a production environment. By the end of the book, you'll have the confidence to choose the right framework for any project and to tackle complex challenges in web development.

A Journey into the Future

The web development world is continuously evolving, with new frameworks and tools emerging at a rapid pace. By mastering the frameworks covered in this book, you will not only be prepared to tackle today's challenges but also position yourself for the future of web development.

In the following chapters, we will explore these frameworks in detail, uncover their strengths and weaknesses, and equip you with the practical skills you need to succeed as a web developer in the modern era.

Let's embark on this exciting journey to mastering web development frameworks and unlock the potential to build fast, scalable, and powerful web applications.

Chapter 1: Introduction to Web Development

The world of web development is a dynamic, ever-evolving landscape, shaped by advancements in technology, design, and user needs. As websites and applications become more sophisticated, the need for efficient development methods, powerful frameworks, and responsive designs has grown. In this chapter, we will explore the **evolution of web development**, the **key concepts** such as front-end and back-end development, and the **importance of web frameworks** in shaping modern web applications.

The Evolution of Web Development

Web development has come a long way since the early days of the internet. Let's take a look at how it has evolved:

1. **The Early Days of the Web (1990s)**:
   o When the web first emerged in the early 1990s, websites were simple, static pages built with **HTML** (HyperText Markup Language) and **CSS** (Cascading Style Sheets) for styling. These early websites were not interactive and did not offer much in terms of functionality beyond basic text and images.
   o At this time, web browsers such as **Netscape Navigator** and **Internet Explorer** were used to

navigate the internet, and web development was limited to basic HTML files, without much emphasis on user interaction or dynamic content.

2. **The Rise of Dynamic Websites (2000s)**:
   - As the internet grew, so did the complexity of websites. The introduction of **JavaScript** allowed for client-side interactivity, enabling websites to respond to user input without reloading the page. This marked the shift from static to **dynamic websites**.
   - The advent of **server-side scripting languages** such as **PHP, ASP.NET**, and **Ruby on Rails** enabled developers to create more dynamic and personalized content. These technologies allowed for the creation of web applications that could interact with databases, manage user accounts, and serve personalized content in real-time.

3. **Responsive Design and Mobile Revolution (2010s)**:
   - With the rise of smartphones and mobile browsing, the need for **responsive web design** became apparent. Websites needed to be optimized for different screen sizes and devices, which led to the adoption of **CSS media queries** and mobile-first development approaches.

- o At this time, **front-end frameworks** like **Bootstrap** and **Foundation** made it easier to design websites that were flexible and adaptable to various screen sizes.
- o The use of **JavaScript libraries** like **jQuery** became widespread, allowing developers to easily add interactive elements and animations to websites.

4. **Modern Web Development (2020s and Beyond)**:
   - o The modern web is now powered by advanced frameworks and technologies that allow for the development of rich, interactive, and highly dynamic applications. Front-end frameworks like **React, Angular**, and **Vue.js** enable developers to create component-based, maintainable, and efficient user interfaces.
   - o **Back-end technologies** have evolved to support **cloud-based architectures**, **microservices**, and **serverless computing**, allowing for scalable and distributed applications.
   - o **Progressive Web Apps (PWAs)** and **single-page applications (SPAs)** have further transformed the way we think about the web, offering app-like experiences directly in the browser.

As web technologies continue to evolve, the role of **web frameworks** has become essential in ensuring that development is efficient, maintainable, and scalable. Frameworks provide the tools and structure necessary to streamline the development process, manage complex applications, and keep up with the ever-growing demands of modern web users.

Key Concepts: Front-End vs Back-End

In web development, there are two primary areas of focus: **front-end** and **back-end**. Both are crucial for building functional and dynamic websites and applications, and understanding the difference between the two is essential for becoming a well-rounded developer.

1. **Front-End Development**:
   - **Front-end** development refers to the part of web development that deals with the user interface (UI) and user experience (UX). It involves everything that users see and interact with directly in the browser. Front-end developers use **HTML, CSS**, and **JavaScript** to build and style websites, ensuring that the site is visually appealing, responsive, and user-friendly.
   - Key technologies used in front-end development:

16

- **HTML**: Provides the structure and content of web pages.
- **CSS**: Styles and lays out the content in an aesthetically pleasing manner.
- **JavaScript**: Adds interactivity, such as form validation, animations, and real-time content updates.

  o **Front-end frameworks** like **React**, **Vue.js**, and **Angular** offer pre-built components and tools that help developers build complex user interfaces more efficiently.

2. **Back-End Development**:

   o **Back-end** development is concerned with the server-side of web applications. It involves creating the logic and functionality that users don't directly interact with but which makes the site work. Back-end developers focus on building databases, managing server communication, and ensuring that data is correctly processed and stored.

   o Key technologies used in back-end development:

     - **Server-side languages**: such as **Node.js**, **Python**, **Ruby**, **PHP**, and **Java**.
     - **Databases**: such as **MySQL**, **PostgreSQL**, **MongoDB**, and **SQLite**.

- **APIs (Application Programming Interfaces)**: used to allow communication between the front-end and back-end of an application.
  - Back-end developers also work on server management, ensuring that applications run efficiently, scale as needed, and can handle large amounts of user data.

In modern web development, **full-stack developers** combine both front-end and back-end development skills, enabling them to build complete applications from start to finish. The ability to work with both front-end and back-end technologies is highly valuable in today's tech industry, as it enables developers to build more comprehensive solutions.

The Importance of Web Frameworks in Modern Web Development

Web frameworks are an essential tool for developers. They provide pre-written code, templates, and libraries that help streamline development and ensure that applications are built using best practices. In modern web development, frameworks have become indispensable for both front-end and back-end development. Here's why they are so important:

1. **Increased Efficiency**:
   - Frameworks help developers save time by providing ready-made solutions for common tasks, such as routing, authentication, and data validation. This means developers don't have to reinvent the wheel each time they start a new project.
   - For example, in **front-end frameworks** like **React** and **Vue.js**, developers can create reusable components that help speed up development and make the codebase easier to maintain.

2. **Code Organization and Structure**:
   - Web frameworks provide a structured way to organize code, making it easier for developers to work collaboratively and maintain code over time. With clear guidelines for code structure, developers can build applications that are more scalable and easier to debug.
   - **Back-end frameworks** like **Express.js**, **Django**, and **Ruby on Rails** provide a well-organized folder structure and modular approach, making the development process smoother and more maintainable.

3. **Security**:
   - Many frameworks come with built-in security features, such as protection against cross-site

scripting (XSS) and SQL injection attacks, which are common vulnerabilities in web applications. These features help developers focus on functionality rather than spending time on securing the application from threats.

o   For instance, **Django** comes with security features like user authentication and protection from cross-site request forgery (CSRF) attacks, which are essential in modern web applications.

4. **Scalability**:

o   Web frameworks are designed to handle applications of varying sizes. By using a framework, developers can ensure that their applications can grow and scale as demand increases. This is especially important for applications that expect a large number of users or need to manage vast amounts of data.

o   **Node.js** and **Express** are examples of frameworks that can handle high-performance and scalable applications, making them popular choices for real-time applications like chat apps and social networks.

5. **Community and Support**:

o   Popular frameworks have large communities of developers who contribute to the framework's development, offer support, and share best practices. This makes it easier for developers to find solutions to problems and stay up-to-date with the latest advancements.

- o For example, **React** has an active community that offers tutorials, tools, and open-source libraries, making it easier for developers to adopt and implement React in their projects.

6. **Cross-Platform Compatibility**:

- o Modern web frameworks, especially front-end frameworks, allow developers to create **responsive** and **cross-platform** applications that work seamlessly on desktops, tablets, and mobile devices. These frameworks include tools that automatically adjust the layout and design of the application based on the user's device.

- o **Bootstrap** and **Tailwind CSS** are popular front-end frameworks that provide a grid system and responsive utilities, allowing developers to create designs that adapt to different screen sizes.

Summary

In this chapter, we've introduced the essential concepts of **web development**, starting with the **evolution of web technologies**, including the rise of dynamic, interactive websites and modern frameworks. We've also explored the key differences between **front-end** and **back-end** development, highlighting the importance of each role in building complete, functional web applications.

Furthermore, we've discussed how **web frameworks** are indispensable in modern web development. They enhance **efficiency**, provide **structure**, improve **security**, and make it easier for developers to create scalable, maintainable applications. Whether you're developing for the front-end with frameworks like **React**, **Vue.js**, or **Angular**, or working on the back-end with **Node.js**, **Express**, or **Django**, understanding and utilizing frameworks is crucial for success in today's web development landscape.

In the following chapters, we will dive deeper into the **various front-end and back-end frameworks**, providing real-world examples and practical knowledge to help you master the technologies used to build **responsive websites** and modern web applications.

Chapter 2: Understanding the Basics of Responsive Design

As more users access the web through a variety of devices, such as smartphones, tablets, and desktops, the need for websites to adjust to different screen sizes and resolutions has never been greater. **Responsive web design** (RWD) has become a fundamental approach for building websites that work seamlessly across devices. In this chapter, we'll explore the concept of **responsive web design**, the **mobile-first approach**, and key techniques for creating responsive websites. We'll also walk through a **real-world example** of building a responsive portfolio site.

What is Responsive Web Design?

Responsive web design is an approach to web design that makes web pages render well on a variety of devices and screen sizes. Instead of designing multiple versions of a website for different devices, responsive design uses a **single design** that automatically adjusts to the screen size and resolution of the device it's viewed on.

Responsive design achieves this by using a combination of flexible grid layouts, media queries, and flexible images. These techniques allow the layout of a website to adapt to different screen widths, ensuring a good user experience on both small mobile devices and large desktop monitors.

Key characteristics of responsive web design include:

- **Fluid Grids**: Content is placed in flexible grid layouts that resize proportionally based on the screen size, rather than using fixed pixel widths.
- **Media Queries**: CSS rules that apply only when certain conditions are met (e.g., when the screen width exceeds 600px), allowing the design to change dynamically based on the device's characteristics.
- **Flexible Images**: Images are sized relative to their containing elements, so they scale down or up depending on the available space.

The goal of responsive design is to provide an optimal viewing experience, ensuring that users can read, navigate, and interact with the content easily across all devices without the need for resizing or horizontal scrolling.

Mobile-First Approach

The **mobile-first approach** is a key philosophy in responsive design, emphasizing the importance of starting the design process with mobile devices in mind. As the use of mobile devices has exploded in recent years, many developers now prioritize designing for **small screens** before expanding to larger ones.

In the mobile-first approach:

1. **Start with small screens**: Begin by designing the layout, functionality, and content for the smallest screen size, ensuring the website is usable and accessible on mobile devices.

2. **Progressively enhance**: Once the mobile layout is in place, use **media queries** to progressively enhance the design for larger screens. This means that desktop or tablet users will get additional features, larger images, or more complex layouts, but mobile users will still have a seamless experience without being overwhelmed by unnecessary elements.

3. **Focus on core content**: On mobile devices, users are often looking for quick, easy access to essential information. A mobile-first design ensures that your website's most important content is visible and accessible without any clutter.

By taking the mobile-first approach, you are catering to the growing number of users who primarily access the web from their smartphones, and you're ensuring that your website is fully optimized for these users before addressing desktop and tablet views.

Key Techniques for Creating Responsive Websites

To effectively implement responsive design, there are several key techniques and best practices that developers and designers can use:

1. **Fluid Grid Layouts**:
    - Instead of using fixed-width layouts with pixel values, responsive web design uses **relative units** like percentages, ems, or rems to define the width of columns, margins, and paddings. This ensures that content adjusts proportionally to the screen size.
    - For example, rather than defining the width of a container as width: 960px, use a percentage such as width: 80% so that it resizes relative to the parent element.

2. **Media Queries**:
    - Media queries are the heart of responsive design. They allow you to apply different CSS styles depending on the characteristics of the device, such as the width of the viewport.
    - Basic syntax for a media query:

    css

    ```
    @media screen and (max-width: 768px) {
    /* Styles for screens smaller than 768px */
    ```

```
.container {
  width: 100%;
  }
}
```

- o You can use media queries to adjust typography, change layouts, and hide or show elements based on screen size, ensuring that the design adapts appropriately to each device.

3. **Flexible Images**:
   - o Images should be sized relative to their containers to prevent them from overflowing or becoming pixelated on larger screens.
   - o Use the max-width: 100% CSS rule to make images responsive, ensuring they scale down to fit the width of their container:

css

```
img {
  max-width: 100%;
  height: auto;
  }
```

4. **Viewport Meta Tag**:
   - o For mobile devices, it's crucial to set the viewport correctly to control the layout's dimensions and

scaling. This is done using the viewport meta tag in the HTML <head> section:

html

```
<meta name="viewport" content="width=device-width, initial-scale=1.0">
```

- o This ensures that the page is scaled correctly to the width of the device, preventing the mobile site from appearing zoomed out or requiring horizontal scrolling.

5. **Responsive Typography**:
    - o Text size should also adapt to different screen sizes. One effective way to make typography responsive is by using **relative units** like em or rem instead of fixed units like px. This allows the font size to scale relative to the root font size or container size.
    - o For example:

css

```
body {
  font-size: 16px;
}
h1 {
  font-size: 2.5rem; /* 2.5 times the root font size */
}
```

6. **Mobile-First Navigation**:

- Navigation menus should be designed to work well on small screens first, and then progressively enhanced for larger screens. A popular technique for mobile navigation is the **hamburger menu**, which hides the navigation links behind a toggle button on smaller screens.
- On larger screens, the navigation can be displayed horizontally or in a more traditional layout.

Real-World Example: Building a Responsive Portfolio Site

Now that we've covered the key techniques for responsive web design, let's apply them to a **real-world example**: building a responsive portfolio site.

A portfolio site is a personal website where you showcase your work, whether it's web development projects, graphic design, photography, or other creative work. The goal is to design the site so it looks great on **desktop**, **tablet**, and **mobile** devices.

Step 1: Setting up the HTML structure
First, we'll set up the basic structure of the portfolio site using HTML:

html

```html
<!DOCTYPE html>
<html lang="en">
<head>
  <meta charset="UTF-8">
  <meta name="viewport" content="width=device-width, initial-scale=1.0">
  <title>Responsive Portfolio</title>
  <link rel="stylesheet" href="styles.css">
</head>
<body>
  <header>
    <nav>
      <ul>
        <li><a href="#about">About Me</a></li>
        <li><a href="#projects">Projects</a></li>
        <li><a href="#contact">Contact</a></li>
      </ul>
    </nav>
  </header>

  <section id="about">
    <h1>About Me</h1>
    <p>Introduction text and biography here.</p>
  </section>

  <section id="projects">
    <h1>My Projects</h1>
    <div class="project-list">
      <!-- Project entries here -->
    </div>
  </section>
```

```
<section id="contact">
  <h1>Contact</h1>
  <p>Contact information or form here.</p>
</section>

<footer>
  <p>&; 2025 My Portfolio</p>
</footer>
</body>
</html>
```

Step 2: Styling with CSS

Next, we'll use **CSS** to style the portfolio site and make it responsive:

css

```
/* Base styles */
body {
  font-family: Arial, sans-serif;
  margin: 0;
  padding: 0;
}

header {
  background-color: #333;
  color: #fff;
  padding: 10px;
}

nav ul {
```

```css
    list-style: none;
    margin: 0;
    padding: 0;
    display: flex;
    justify-content: center;
}

nav ul li {
  margin: 0 20px;
}

nav ul li a {
  color: #fff;
  text-decoration: none;
}

section {
  padding: 20px;
}

.project-list {
  display: grid;
  grid-template-columns: repeat(auto-fill, minmax(300px, 1fr));
  gap: 20px;
}

/* Responsive styles */
@media screen and (max-width: 768px) {
  header {
    padding: 15px;
```

```
}

nav ul {
  flex-direction: column;
  align-items: center;
}

.project-list {
  grid-template-columns: 1fr;
}
}
```

In this example:

1. We used **CSS grid** to create a responsive layout for the project section, where the number of columns changes based on the screen width.

2. The **media query** adjusts the layout for smaller screens (under 768px), switching the navigation to a vertical layout and making the projects section a single-column grid.

3. The **viewport meta tag** ensures that the site scales appropriately on mobile devices.

By following these steps, we've created a **responsive portfolio website** that adapts to both large desktop screens and smaller mobile devices.

Summary

In this chapter, we've covered the basics of **responsive web design**, including its definition, techniques, and importance in modern web development. We introduced the **mobile-first approach**, which prioritizes mobile design before expanding to larger screen sizes. Key techniques like **fluid grids**, **media queries**, **flexible images**, and **responsive typography** allow web developers to create websites that perform well across devices.

Through a real-world example, we demonstrated how to build a **responsive portfolio site**, showcasing the practical application of the concepts discussed. With these tools and techniques, you're now equipped to create websites that deliver an optimal user experience across all screen sizes and devices.

Chapter 3: The Role of Web Development Frameworks

In modern web development, frameworks have become essential tools for building efficient, scalable, and maintainable websites and web applications. A **web development framework** is a pre-built collection of libraries, tools, and best practices that help developers structure and streamline the development process. Frameworks provide a foundation for creating applications, making it easier to tackle complex tasks such as routing, database management, security, and user authentication.

In this chapter, we'll explore the **role of web development frameworks**, the **benefits of using a framework**, and the differences between **front-end** and **back-end** frameworks, as well as some examples of each.

Why Use a Web Framework?

When building a website or web application, you have two options: you can either start from scratch and build everything yourself, or you can leverage a web development framework. Here are some reasons why using a framework is highly recommended:

1. **Faster Development**:

- o Frameworks provide pre-built solutions for common tasks, such as form validation, authentication, and database connections. By using a framework, you don't have to reinvent the wheel for every project. This can significantly speed up development and allow you to focus on the unique aspects of your application.
- o For example, if you're building a blog, a framework like **Django** will give you built-in tools for handling user authentication, managing posts, and serving templates.

2. **Consistency**:
   - o Frameworks enforce **best practices** and **design patterns**, which ensures that your code is consistent across the project. This is particularly important when working with teams, as it ensures everyone is following the same guidelines.
   - o Frameworks also help in managing the **file structure** and **coding standards**, making it easier to collaborate on large projects.

3. **Security**:
   - o Security is a crucial aspect of web development, and frameworks often come with built-in security features to help protect your application from common vulnerabilities like **SQL injection, cross-**

site scripting **(XSS)**, and **cross-site request forgery (CSRF)**.

o For example, **Rails** provides automatic protection against SQL injection by using **ActiveRecord** to interact with the database, while **Django** includes features like protection against CSRF attacks and **secure password hashing** out-of-the-box.

4. **Maintainability**:

o Frameworks are designed to make it easier to maintain and update your code. By adhering to specific conventions and structure, frameworks ensure that your code is clean, organized, and modular.

o In the long run, this makes it easier to add new features, fix bugs, or scale the application without causing chaos in the codebase.

5. **Community Support and Documentation**:

o Popular frameworks have large, active communities that provide extensive resources, such as **tutorials**, **documentation**, and **support forums**. This makes it easier to find solutions to problems and get assistance from experienced developers.

o For example, **React** has a vast community that regularly publishes libraries, tools, and tutorials, which can greatly speed up development and problem-solving.

Benefits of Using a Framework in Web Development

Let's dive deeper into the specific **benefits** of using a web development framework:

1. **Improved Efficiency**:
   - Web development frameworks save developers time by providing reusable components and built-in functionalities. Developers don't need to code everything from scratch; instead, they can use the pre-existing tools offered by the framework to speed up the development process.
   - For instance, a framework like **Vue.js** simplifies building interactive user interfaces, and **Express.js** helps set up routing and server-side logic in a fraction of the time it would take without a framework.

2. **Modularity and Reusability**:
   - Frameworks encourage modular development, where different parts of the application are developed in isolation and can be reused in different parts of the project or even in future projects.

o In front-end development, for example, **React** allows developers to build small, reusable components like buttons, forms, and navigation menus, which can be easily combined to form complex UIs.

3. **Built-In Tools**:

o Most web frameworks come with integrated tools for tasks such as **routing, templating, authentication, database access**, and **session management**. These tools reduce the amount of boilerplate code you have to write and provide a standard approach to common development tasks.

o For example, **Laravel** for PHP provides built-in routing, authentication, and **Eloquent ORM** for working with databases, allowing developers to focus more on the business logic than infrastructure.

4. **Scalability**:

o Web development frameworks are built to support the growth of applications. They provide scalable solutions that can handle increasing traffic, larger datasets, and more complex functionalities as your application grows.

o **Node.js**, combined with the **Express** framework, can handle a large number of concurrent connections efficiently, making it ideal for building scalable, real-time applications like chat apps or live-streaming platforms.

5. **Cross-Browser Compatibility**:

   o Many frameworks, particularly front-end frameworks, are designed to handle cross-browser compatibility issues. They ensure that your website works smoothly across different browsers and devices, saving time spent on testing and fixing compatibility bugs.

   o **Bootstrap** is a great example of a front-end framework that handles responsiveness and browser compatibility automatically.

Types of Web Frameworks: Front-End vs Back-End

Web development frameworks can be broadly classified into two categories: **front-end frameworks** and **back-end frameworks**. Let's break down the differences and the role each type of framework plays in the development process.

1. **Front-End Frameworks**:

   o **Front-end frameworks** focus on the user interface (UI) and user experience (UX). They provide tools for creating and managing the visual aspects of a website or application, including layout, styling, interactivity, and animations.

o These frameworks typically provide:

- **Pre-designed UI components**: Buttons, modals, carousels, etc.

- **Grid systems**: To help create flexible and responsive layouts.

- **Interactivity tools**: JavaScript-based components for handling dynamic content (e.g., form validation, image sliders, etc.).

o Some popular front-end frameworks include:

- **React**: A JavaScript library for building user interfaces, known for its component-based structure and efficiency in rendering updates.

- **Vue.js**: A progressive JavaScript framework for building UIs and single-page applications, with a simple and flexible architecture.

- **Angular**: A full-featured framework by Google for building complex, large-scale single-page applications (SPAs).

- **Bootstrap**: A CSS framework that provides responsive grid systems, pre-designed UI components, and JavaScript tools for building mobile-first websites.

2. **Back-End Frameworks**:

o **Back-end frameworks** handle the server-side logic and manage interactions with databases, APIs, and other back-end services. These frameworks provide a structured way to manage and process data, implement business logic, and ensure the security of web applications.

o Common features of back-end frameworks include:

- **Routing**: Handling user requests and directing them to the appropriate server-side function.

- **Authentication and authorization**: Managing user sessions and restricting access to protected resources.

- **Database management**: Connecting to and interacting with databases, typically using Object-Relational Mapping (ORM) tools.

- **API support**: Building and handling RESTful APIs for interaction between the server and the client.

o Some popular back-end frameworks include:

- **Node.js + Express**: A lightweight and fast back-end framework for building web servers and APIs using JavaScript.

- **Django**: A Python-based framework that emphasizes rapid development and follows the "batteries-included" philosophy, providing everything you need to build a web application.

- **Ruby on Rails**: A full-stack framework for building dynamic, database-driven web applications using Ruby.
- **Laravel**: A PHP framework known for its elegant syntax and tools for tasks like routing, authentication, and database interaction.

Summary

Web development frameworks play a pivotal role in building modern websites and web applications. In this chapter, we discussed the importance of using a framework to **improve development efficiency**, **ensure security**, and **enhance scalability**. Frameworks provide built-in tools that handle common tasks, save time, and enforce best practices.

We also explored the distinction between **front-end** and **back-end** **frameworks**. **Front-end frameworks** are designed to manage the user interface and enhance the user experience, while **back-end frameworks** focus on server-side functionality, database interaction, and business logic.

By leveraging the power of web development frameworks, developers can focus on building great user experiences, solving business problems, and scaling applications, all while reducing the complexity of web development. In the following chapters, we will dive deeper into specific front-end and back-end frameworks, giving you the tools and techniques to build modern, responsive web applications.

Chapter 4: Introduction to Front-End Frameworks

In web development, the **front-end** refers to everything that users interact with directly in their web browsers. It's responsible for how a website looks, feels, and behaves, and it includes the layout, design, structure, and interactivity of the site. As web applications have become more complex, **front-end frameworks** have emerged as essential tools for simplifying and streamlining the development process.

In this chapter, we will explore the role and significance of **front-end frameworks**, identify the qualities that make a framework effective, and provide a **real-world example** of building a simple landing page using a front-end framework.

Overview of Front-End Frameworks

A **front-end framework** is a pre-prepared collection of code that provides a structure for building the front-end of web applications. These frameworks typically consist of HTML, CSS, and JavaScript, as well as additional tools, components, and libraries that allow developers to create user interfaces with greater ease and efficiency.

Some of the most popular front-end frameworks include:

1. **React**:
   - A JavaScript library developed by Facebook for building **user interfaces** (UIs). React follows a **component-based architecture**, where each part of the UI is broken down into individual, reusable components.
   - React is known for its **virtual DOM** (Document Object Model) that optimizes rendering and improves performance.

2. **Vue.js**:
   - A progressive JavaScript framework for building UIs and single-page applications (SPAs). Vue focuses on being **incrementally adoptable**, meaning that you can start with small components and scale up to more complex applications as needed.
   - Vue.js is loved for its simplicity, ease of integration, and lightweight nature.

3. **Angular**:
   - A full-fledged JavaScript framework maintained by Google. Angular is designed for building large-scale, **dynamic web applications**. It uses **two-way data binding** and **dependency injection** to create powerful, scalable applications.
   - Angular includes everything a developer needs for building a complete front-end app, including routing,

forms management, HTTP client, and state management.

4. **Bootstrap**:
   o A front-end framework that provides a set of **CSS and JavaScript** tools for building responsive, mobile-first websites. Bootstrap includes ready-to-use components such as navigation bars, buttons, grids, and form elements, making it an excellent choice for developers who need to rapidly prototype designs.

5. **Foundation**:
   o Developed by ZURB, Foundation is a flexible front-end framework that provides a responsive grid system and pre-designed UI components. It's used for building responsive, mobile-first web applications and is known for being **customizable**.

These frameworks help developers build web applications with speed and efficiency by providing pre-built, reusable code and tools. By using a front-end framework, developers can focus more on **custom functionality** rather than spending time on repetitive tasks like setting up grid systems or handling browser compatibility issues.

What Makes a Front-End Framework Effective?

To build effective, scalable, and maintainable web applications, a front-end framework must meet several key criteria. The following qualities are what make a front-end framework truly effective:

1. **Modularity and Reusability**:
   - The framework should allow developers to build small, **reusable components** that can be combined to create complex UIs. Components are the building blocks of modern front-end frameworks like React and Vue.js. With modular components, developers can maintain and update code more efficiently.

2. **Responsive Design**:
   - A good front-end framework should help developers create responsive designs that work seamlessly across different screen sizes and devices. Features like **grid systems**, **media queries**, and **flexbox** are important for ensuring that websites and applications look good on desktops, tablets, and mobile devices.

3. **Performance Optimization**:
   - The framework should offer built-in performance optimization techniques such as **virtual DOM** (in React) or lazy loading of components. Optimized performance ensures that the application runs smoothly and efficiently, even as it grows in complexity.

4. **Developer Tools and Ecosystem**:

   o A strong front-end framework should be accompanied by a rich ecosystem of **developer tools**, **libraries**, and **plugins** that make development faster and easier. For example, React has **React DevTools** for debugging, and Vue has tools for state management and routing.

5. **Clear Documentation and Active Community**:

   o A comprehensive, well-organized **documentation** is essential for developers to quickly learn and effectively use the framework. Additionally, an active community can provide support, tutorials, and third-party tools, making it easier for developers to troubleshoot issues and stay up-to-date with the latest advancements.

6. **Scalability and Flexibility**:

   o The framework should be scalable enough to handle large applications and flexible enough to allow for customizations. For instance, Angular's modular approach makes it suitable for building enterprise-level applications, while React and Vue.js allow for incremental adoption, meaning they can be used for everything from small websites to complex SPAs.

7. **Cross-Browser Compatibility**:

○   A framework should ensure that the web application works consistently across all major browsers (e.g., Chrome, Firefox, Safari, Edge). This reduces the time spent on fixing browser compatibility issues, ensuring a seamless user experience.

Real-World Example: Building a Simple Landing Page Using a Front-End Framework

Now that we understand the importance of front-end frameworks, let's walk through a **real-world example** of building a **simple landing page** using a front-end framework. We will use **React** for this example because of its widespread use and component-based architecture.

1. **Step 1: Set Up the Development Environment**

    ○   First, we need to set up our development environment by installing **Node.js** and **npm** (Node Package Manager). Then, we create a new React project using **Create React App**, a tool that sets up the boilerplate for a React application.

    bash

    ```
    npx create-react-app landing-page
    cd landing-page
    ```

npm start

2. **Step 2: Plan the Landing Page Layout**

   o We will design a simple landing page with:

      ▪ A **header** section with a navigation bar.

      ▪ A **hero** section with a call-to-action (CTA) button.

      ▪ A **features** section with brief descriptions.

      ▪ A **footer** with links and right information.

3. **Step 3: Create Reusable Components**

   o In React, we break down the layout into components. We create the following components:

      ▪ **Header**: Contains the navigation bar.

      ▪ **Hero**: Contains the title, description, and CTA button.

      ▪ **Features**: Lists the key features of the product or service.

      ▪ **Footer**: Contains right information and links.

   Example of the **Header component**:

   jsx

   ```
   import React from 'react';

   function Header() {
    return (
     <header>
   ```

```
  <nav>
   <ul>
    <li><a href="#hero">Home</a></li>
    <li><a href="#features">Features</a></li>
    <li><a href="#contact">Contact</a></li>
   </ul>
  </nav>
 </header>
);
}
```

export default Header;

4. **Step 4: Add Styling Using CSS**

   o We use **CSS** to style the components and ensure the landing page is responsive. We can use **CSS Flexbox** or **CSS Grid** to create the layout. To make the page responsive, we add media queries to adjust the layout for different screen sizes.

css

```
/* Global styles */
body {
  font-family: Arial, sans-serif;
  margin: 0;
  padding: 0;
}
```

```css
header {
  background-color: #333;
  color: #fff;
  padding: 20px;
}

nav ul {
  list-style: none;
  display: flex;
  justify-content: center;
}

nav ul li {
  margin: 0 15px;
}

nav ul li a {
  color: white;
  text-decoration: none;
}

@media (max-width: 768px) {
  header {
    padding: 15px;
  }

  nav ul {
    flex-direction: column;
  }
}
```

5. **Step 5: Assemble the Components**

   o Now, we can assemble all the components into our main App component. The App component will include the **Header**, **Hero**, **Features**, and **Footer** components, and render them in the correct order.

   Example of the **App component**:

   jsx

```
import React from 'react';
import Header from './Header';
import Hero from './Hero';
import Features from './Features';
import Footer from './Footer';

function App() {
  return (
    <div>
      <Header />
      <Hero />
      <Features />
      <Footer />
    </div>
  );
}

export default App;
```

6. **Step 6: Run and Test the Landing Page**

○ Once we have assembled all the components and added the necessary styles, we can run the project using npm start to launch the app in the browser. The landing page should be responsive, adjusting to different screen sizes as you resize the browser window.

Summary

In this chapter, we introduced **front-end frameworks**, specifically **React**, and discussed why they are essential for modern web development. We explored the **benefits** of using a framework, such as faster development, modularity, performance optimization, and enhanced security. A good front-end framework simplifies complex tasks and provides tools for building responsive, scalable, and maintainable web applications.

We also walked through a **real-world example** of building a **simple landing page** using React. This example highlighted how to use **React components**, **CSS** for styling, and **media queries** to ensure the page is responsive. By using a front-end framework like React, we were able to efficiently build a modern, dynamic, and responsive website.

In the following chapters, we will delve deeper into various front-end frameworks and explore how to harness their full potential to create sophisticated web applications.

Chapter 5: Mastering HTML and CSS

In web development, **HTML** (HyperText Markup Language) and **CSS** (Cascading Style Sheets) form the foundation of every website. While HTML provides the structure and content of a web page, CSS controls its visual appearance. To create modern, responsive websites, it's important to master both HTML5 and CSS3, using best practices to ensure accessibility, SEO (Search Engine Optimization), and responsiveness.

In this chapter, we will cover **best practices** in **HTML5** and **CSS3**, the importance of **semantic HTML** for **accessibility** and **SEO**, as well as how to use **Flexbox** and **CSS Grid Layout** for responsive design. We will also walk through a **real-world example** of crafting a **responsive grid layout** with **Flexbox**.

Best Practices in HTML5 and CSS3

To build modern, maintainable, and scalable websites, it's crucial to follow **best practices** in both **HTML5** and **CSS3**.

1. **HTML5 Best Practices**:
   - **Use semantic elements**: Use HTML5's semantic elements like <header>, <footer>, <article>, <section>, and <nav> to structure your page. This helps make the code more readable, maintainable, and accessible.

- o **Validate HTML**: Always validate your HTML code to avoid errors. Use **W3C HTML Validator** to ensure the code adheres to web standards.

- o **Avoid inline styles**: Instead of writing styles directly in HTML with the style attribute, define your styles in separate CSS files. This improves maintainability and separates structure from presentation.

- o **Ensure proper use of forms**: Use appropriate form elements such as <input>, <label>, <textarea>, and <button> to ensure a better user experience and accessibility.

- o **Use alt attribute for images**: Always provide descriptive **alt text** for images using the alt attribute. This helps screen readers describe the image for visually impaired users and improves SEO.

2. **CSS3 Best Practices**:

- o **Use external stylesheets**: Always link to external stylesheets using the <link> tag in the HTML <head>. This keeps your code organized and reusable.

- o **Organize CSS rules**: Organize your CSS by grouping related rules together. You can use tools like **Preprocessors** (e.g., **SASS**, **LESS**) to organize styles more efficiently and reduce duplication.

- o **Avoid CSS shorthand excessively**: While shorthand is a convenient way to write styles, avoid overusing it as it can reduce readability and make debugging more difficult.

- o **Use rem and em units instead of** px: For font sizes and layout dimensions, use **relative units** like rem (relative to the root element) and em (relative to the parent element) instead of px to improve scalability and accessibility.
- o **Mobile-first design**: Start designing your site for mobile screens first, and then progressively enhance the design for larger screens using **media queries**.

Semantic HTML for Accessibility and SEO

Semantic HTML refers to the use of HTML elements that clearly describe their meaning both in the context of the page and the wider web. Using semantic elements correctly improves **accessibility**, ensures **better SEO**, and helps developers maintain cleaner, more understandable code.

1. **Accessibility**:
   - o **Semantic HTML elements** improve accessibility by helping assistive technologies (such as screen readers) interpret the content of a web page correctly. For example, the <article> element indicates content

that can stand alone, and a screen reader will announce it as such, giving users a better experience.

- o **Proper heading structure**: Use heading tags (`<h1>`, `<h2>`, etc.) in a logical, hierarchical order. This helps users with screen readers navigate through the content and improves SEO.
- o **Forms**: Use the `<label>` element correctly to associate form labels with their respective form controls. This allows screen readers to accurately announce the purpose of form fields.
- o **Descriptive links and buttons**: Use meaningful text for links and buttons (e.g., `<a href="#">Learn More</a>` instead of `<a href="#">Click Here</a>`). Descriptive links provide more context to users, especially those with disabilities.

2. **SEO**:

- o **Use of headings**: Properly structured headings (`<h1>`, `<h2>`, etc.) are important for SEO because they define the hierarchy of content. Search engines use headings to understand the structure of your content and improve ranking.
- o **Alt attributes for images**: Descriptive alt text for images allows search engines to index them properly, improving image search rankings and accessibility for visually impaired users.

o **Avoid unnecessary divs**: Excessive use of non-semantic elements like <div> and <span> can negatively impact SEO. Whenever possible, use semantic elements that better describe the content, such as <article>, <section>, or <header>.

By using semantic HTML, you ensure that your website is not only accessible to users with disabilities but also optimized for search engines, ultimately enhancing both user experience and SEO rankings.

Flexbox and Grid Layout for Responsive Design

Responsive web design ensures that your website looks great on all screen sizes, from desktop monitors to mobile phones. **CSS Flexbox** and **CSS Grid Layout** are two powerful layout techniques for creating flexible and responsive designs.

1. **Flexbox**:
   o **CSS Flexbox** is a one-dimensional layout system designed to distribute space along a row or column. It helps you align and distribute space among items in a container, even when their sizes are unknown or dynamic.
   o Key properties in Flexbox:
      ▪ **display: flex**: Defines a flex container.

- **justify-content**: Aligns items horizontally (e.g., center, space-between).
- **align-items**: Aligns items vertically (e.g., center, stretch).
- **flex-direction**: Specifies the direction of flex items (e.g., row, column).
- **flex-wrap**: Allows flex items to wrap onto the next line if necessary.

Flexbox is ideal for small-scale layouts where elements need to be aligned and spaced evenly within a container, such as navigation bars or form layouts.

2. **Grid Layout**:
   - **CSS Grid Layout** is a two-dimensional layout system that allows you to create complex grid-based designs, with both rows and columns. It's perfect for more complex, large-scale layouts like entire page structures.
   - Key properties in Grid Layout:
     - **display: grid**: Defines a grid container.
     - **grid-template-columns**: Specifies the number and size of columns.
     - **grid-template-rows**: Specifies the number and size of rows.

- **grid-column and grid-row**: Define how grid items span across columns and rows.
- **gap**: Specifies the space between grid items.

Grid Layout is best for building complex, responsive layouts where precise control over both rows and columns is needed.

Real-World Example: Crafting a Responsive Grid Layout with Flexbox

Let's apply the concepts we've discussed by building a **responsive grid layout** using **Flexbox**.

We'll create a simple grid layout for a portfolio page, where each portfolio item is displayed in a flexible grid container. The layout will adjust based on the screen size.

Step 1: HTML Structure

html

```
<!DOCTYPE html>
<html lang="en">
<head>
  <meta charset="UTF-8">
  <meta name="viewport" content="width=device-width, initial-scale=1.0">
  <title>Portfolio</title>
  <link rel="stylesheet" href="styles.css">
</head>
```

```html
<body>
 <header>
  <h1>My Portfolio</h1>
 </header>

 <section class="portfolio">
  <div class="portfolio-item">Project 1</div>
  <div class="portfolio-item">Project 2</div>
  <div class="portfolio-item">Project 3</div>
  <div class="portfolio-item">Project 4</div>
  <div class="portfolio-item">Project 5</div>
  <div class="portfolio-item">Project 6</div>
 </section>

 <footer>
  <p>&; 2025 My Portfolio</p>
 </footer>
</body>
</html>
```

Step 2: CSS Styling

css

```css
/* Global styles */
body {
 font-family: Arial, sans-serif;
 margin: 0;
 padding: 0;
 background-color: #f9f9f9;
}
```

```css
header {
  text-align: center;
  padding: 20px;
  background-color: #333;
  color: white;
}

h1 {
  margin: 0;
}

footer {
  text-align: center;
  padding: 10px;
  background-color: #333;
  color: white;
}

/* Portfolio styles */
.portfolio {
  display: flex;
  flex-wrap: wrap;
  justify-content: space-around;
  margin: 20px;
}

.portfolio-item {
  background-color: #fff;
  border: 1px solid #ddd;
```

```
  padding: 20px;
  margin: 10px;
  flex: 1 1 calc(33% - 20px); /* Flex item takes up 33% width, accounting for
spacing */
  box-sizing: border-box;
  text-align: center;
  transition: transform 0.3s;
}


.portfolio-item:hover {
  transform: scale(1.05);
}


/* Responsive styles */
@media (max-width: 768px) {
  .portfolio-item {
    flex: 1 1 calc(50% - 20px); /* On smaller screens, each item takes up 50% of
the container width */
  }
}


@media (max-width: 480px) {
  .portfolio-item {
    flex: 1 1 100%; /* On very small screens, each item takes up the full width */
  }
}
```

Step 3: Explanation

- The .portfolio container uses display: flex to enable the flex layout. The flex-wrap: wrap property ensures that portfolio items wrap to the next line when there isn't enough space on the current line.

- Each .portfolio-item is set to take up 33% of the container's width (flex: 1 1 calc(33% - 20px)) on large screens, with 20px subtracted to account for spacing between items.

- For **smaller screens**, media queries adjust the layout: at 768px, each item takes up 50% of the container's width, and at 480px or smaller, each item takes up the full width.

Summary

In this chapter, we covered the essentials of **HTML5** and **CSS3**, including best practices for building well-structured, maintainable, and accessible websites. We explored the importance of **semantic HTML** for **accessibility** and **SEO**, and how to use **Flexbox** and **CSS Grid Layout** to create flexible, responsive designs.

We also walked through a **real-world example** of creating a responsive portfolio layout using **Flexbox**, demonstrating how to build a grid system that adapts to different screen sizes.

By mastering these fundamental techniques, you'll be well-equipped to build modern, responsive, and accessible websites that work seamlessly across a wide range of devices

Chapter 6: Introduction to JavaScript and DOM Manipulation

JavaScript is a fundamental programming language that enables developers to add interactivity, manipulate web page content, and manage data in web applications. It is a key part of the **frontend development** stack, alongside **HTML** and **CSS**. When combined with the **Document Object Model (DOM)**, JavaScript enables developers to dynamically interact with and update the structure, style, and content of web pages.

In this chapter, we will explore an **overview of JavaScript**, the **Document Object Model (DOM)**, and how JavaScript can be used to manipulate the DOM to create dynamic and interactive web experiences. Finally, we will walk through a **real-world example** of building a **dynamic to-do list** application that allows users to add, delete, and mark tasks as complete.

Overview of JavaScript

JavaScript is a **high-level, interpreted programming language** used primarily for creating interactive effects and dynamic content on websites. It runs in the browser and enables developers to manipulate HTML and CSS on the fly, responding to user input, API requests, and other events.

Key features of JavaScript:

1. **Event-driven**: JavaScript allows developers to define functions that respond to events, such as clicks, mouse movements, or keyboard inputs. For example, a JavaScript function can be triggered when a user clicks a button, submitting a form, or hovering over an image.

2. **Client-side scripting**: JavaScript runs directly in the browser, meaning it doesn't require communication with a web server to execute, making it fast and efficient for client-side interactions.

3. **Manipulation of the DOM**: JavaScript can dynamically change the structure of a web page by interacting with the DOM (the HTML structure) in real-time, allowing for updates and changes without needing to reload the page.

4. **Asynchronous programming**: JavaScript supports asynchronous operations, such as **AJAX** (Asynchronous JavaScript and XML), enabling developers to load data in the background and update the page without refreshing the whole site.

In modern web development, JavaScript is essential for building **single-page applications (SPAs)**, handling **form validation**, performing **animations**, and interacting with web APIs.

The Document Object Model (DOM)

The **Document Object Model (DOM)** is a programming interface for web documents. It represents the structure of an HTML or XML document as a tree of **nodes**, where each node corresponds to a part of the document (such as an element, attribute, or text).

For example, consider this simple HTML structure:

html

```
<!DOCTYPE html>
<html>
 <body>
  <h1>Welcome to My Website</h1>
  <p>This is a paragraph.</p>
  <button id="changeTextButton">Click me</button>
 </body>
</html>
```

The DOM represents this HTML as a tree-like structure, where each element is a node:

css

Document

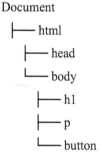

```
Document
 ├── html
 │    ├── head
 │    └── body
 │         ├── h1
 │         ├── p
 │         └── button
```

With JavaScript, you can access and manipulate this DOM structure to make dynamic changes to the content, attributes, or style of the webpage.

Key DOM manipulation concepts:

1. **Accessing elements**: JavaScript provides various methods to access elements in the DOM, such as document.getElementById(), document.querySelector(), and document.querySelectorAll().

2. **Modifying elements**: Once elements are selected, JavaScript can modify them by changing their **text content**, **attributes**, or **CSS styles**. For example, you can change the text of a paragraph or the background color of a div.

3. **Event handling**: JavaScript allows you to add event listeners to DOM elements, enabling actions like button clicks or mouse movements to trigger JavaScript functions.

Manipulating the DOM with JavaScript

Now that we have an understanding of what the DOM is, let's explore how JavaScript can interact with it. Below are some common tasks JavaScript can perform on the DOM:

1. **Selecting DOM Elements**:

o To manipulate an element, you first need to **select** it. You can select elements using various methods:

- document.getElementById(id) – Selects an element by its ID.
- document.querySelector(selector) – Selects the first element that matches the given CSS selector.
- document.querySelectorAll(selector) – Selects all elements that match the given CSS selector.

Example:

javascript

```
const heading = document.getElementById('heading');
const paragraph = document.querySelector('p');
```

2. **Modifying Content**:
   o After selecting an element, you can change its content using JavaScript:
   - element.innerHTML – Changes the HTML content inside an element.
   - element.textContent – Changes the text content inside an element.

Example:

javascript

```
heading.textContent = 'Hello, JavaScript!';
paragraph.innerHTML = 'This is <strong>dynamic</strong> content.';
```

3. **Modifying Attributes**:

   o JavaScript can modify an element's attributes using methods like setAttribute() and getAttribute():

   javascript

```
const button = document.getElementById('changeTextButton');
button.setAttribute('disabled', 'true');  // Disable the button
console.log(button.getAttribute('id'));  // Logs 'changeTextButton'
```

4. **Adding Event Listeners**:

   o You can make elements interactive by adding **event listeners** that trigger specific functions when certain events occur, such as clicks or form submissions.

   javascript

```
const button = document.getElementById('changeTextButton');
button.addEventListener('click', function() {
  alert('Button clicked!');
});
```

Real-World Example: Building a Dynamic To-Do List

Let's now apply the concepts we've learned to build a **dynamic to-do list** application. This app allows users to add, delete, and mark tasks as completed, demonstrating how to use JavaScript to manipulate the DOM and create interactivity.

Step 1: HTML Structure

html

```html
<!DOCTYPE html>
<html lang="en">
<head>
  <meta charset="UTF-8">
  <meta name="viewport" content="width=device-width, initial-scale=1.0">
  <title>To-Do List</title>
  <link rel="stylesheet" href="styles.css">
</head>
<body>
  <h1>To-Do List</h1>
  <input type="text" id="newTask" placeholder="Add a new task">
  <button id="addTaskButton">Add Task</button>

  <ul id="taskList">
    <!-- Tasks will appear here -->
  </ul>

  <script src="script.js"></script>
</body>
</html>
```

Step 2: CSS Styling

css

```css
/* Basic styling */
body {
  font-family: Arial, sans-serif;
  margin: 20px;
}

h1 {
  text-align: center;
}

#taskList {
  list-style-type: none;
  padding: 0;
}

li {
  padding: 10px;
  margin: 5px;
  background-color: #f4f4f4;
  border-radius: 5px;
}

.completed {
  text-decoration: line-through;
  color: gray;
}

button {
```

```css
  padding: 5px 10px;
  background-color: #4CAF50;
  color: white;
  border: none;
  cursor: pointer;
}

button:hover {
  background-color: #45a049;
}
```

Step 3: JavaScript (DOM Manipulation)

javascript

```javascript
// Get elements from the DOM
const taskInput = document.getElementById('newTask');
const addButton = document.getElementById('addTaskButton');
const taskList = document.getElementById('taskList');

// Function to add a new task
function addTask() {
  const taskText = taskInput.value;

  if (taskText.trim() !== '') {
    // Create a new list item
    const newTask = document.createElement('li');
    newTask.textContent = taskText;

    // Add event listener to mark task as complete
    newTask.addEventListener('click', () => {
```

```
newTask.classList.toggle('completed');
});

// Add event listener to delete task
newTask.addEventListener('dblclick', () => {
  taskList.removeChild(newTask);
});

// Append the new task to the list
taskList.appendChild(newTask);

// Clear the input field
taskInput.value = '';
  }
}

// Add event listener to add button
addButton.addEventListener('click', addTask);

// Optional: Add a press 'Enter' functionality to add tasks
taskInput.addEventListener('keypress', function(event) {
  if (event.key === 'Enter') {
    addTask();
  }
});
```

Explanation:

- **HTML**: We create an input field for entering tasks, a button to add tasks, and an unordered list (<ul>) to display the tasks.

- **CSS**: We add some basic styles for the page layout and also a .completed class that strikes through the text when a task is marked as completed.
- **JavaScript**:
  - We use getElementById to access the input field, button, and task list.
  - The addTask function is triggered when the "Add Task" button is clicked. It creates a new <li> element, adds text content to it, and appends it to the task list.
  - Each task has two event listeners:
    - One to toggle the completed class when clicked (marking it as completed or undone).
    - One to remove the task when it is double-clicked.
  - The input field is cleared after a task is added.

Summary

In this chapter, we introduced **JavaScript** and its role in web development, emphasizing its ability to add interactivity to web pages. We also explored the **Document Object Model (DOM)**, which represents the structure of a webpage, and how JavaScript can be used to manipulate it.

We discussed key methods for interacting with the DOM, such as selecting elements, modifying content, adding event listeners, and handling user input. Finally, we built a **dynamic to-do list** application that demonstrates how JavaScript can be used to create a real-time, interactive web experience by manipulating the DOM.

By mastering JavaScript and DOM manipulation, you can create highly interactive and dynamic web pages that respond to user input and make the web a more engaging experience.

Chapter 7: Introduction to Front-End Frameworks: React

React has become one of the most popular front-end frameworks for building dynamic and interactive user interfaces. Developed and maintained by **Facebook**, React provides a powerful yet simple way to create reusable UI components that can efficiently update and render data in response to user interactions. Its component-based architecture and emphasis on virtual DOM make React an ideal choice for building modern web applications.

In this chapter, we will introduce you to **React**, its core concepts like **JSX syntax, components**, and **props**, as well as how **state management** and **lifecycle methods** work in React. We will also walk through a **real-world example** of creating a simple **React-based weather app**.

What is React and Why Use It?

React is a **JavaScript library** for building user interfaces. It enables developers to build complex and interactive UIs with a focus on **simplicity** and **performance**. React is widely used for building single-page applications (SPAs), where the user experience is highly dynamic and the page doesn't need to reload when interacting with the content.

Here's why you should use React:

1. **Component-Based Architecture**:
   - o React encourages developers to break the UI down into **reusable components**. Each component is responsible for rendering part of the user interface, and can be reused throughout the application.
   - o This component-based architecture promotes **modularity**, **scalability**, and **maintainability**. You can create smaller, isolated components and combine them to build more complex UIs.

2. **Virtual DOM**:
   - o React uses a **virtual DOM** to efficiently manage updates to the user interface. When a user interacts with a React app, React first updates the virtual DOM, compares it to the real DOM, and then applies only the necessary changes. This results in faster updates and better performance compared to traditional DOM manipulation.

3. **Declarative Syntax**:
   - o React allows you to describe how the UI should look for any given state, and it will handle the updates for you. Instead of imperatively manipulating the DOM (e.g., using jQuery), React allows you to simply

declare what the UI should look like, and React takes care of the rest.

4. **Strong Ecosystem and Community**:

    o   React has a large and active community that contributes to a rich ecosystem of **third-party libraries, tools**, and **resources**. Whether you need to add routing (via **React Router**) or manage global state (via **Redux**), the React ecosystem provides a variety of solutions that fit your needs.

JSX Syntax, Components, and Props

JSX (JavaScript XML) is a syntax extension to JavaScript that allows you to write HTML-like code inside JavaScript. JSX makes it easier to describe the structure of the user interface in a familiar format while still taking full advantage of JavaScript's power.

1. **JSX Syntax**:

    o   JSX allows you to write HTML-like elements and components in your JavaScript code. It looks similar to HTML but is more powerful because it can contain JavaScript expressions.

    o   For example:

    jsx

```
const element = <h1>Hello, World!</h1>;
```

Here, element is a JSX expression that will render an <h1> tag with the text "Hello, World!" when the component is rendered.

2. **Components**:

- o React applications are built using **components**, which are reusable, self-contained units of the UI. A component can be a simple **function** or a **class** that returns JSX to describe what should appear on the screen.

- o There are two types of components:

  - ▪ **Functional Components**: These are simple JavaScript functions that return JSX.

    jsx

    ```jsx
    function MyComponent() {
      return <h1>Welcome to React!</h1>;
    }
    ```

  - ▪ **Class Components**: These are ES6 classes that extend React.Component and can hold additional functionality like **state** and **lifecycle methods**.

    jsx

```
class MyComponent extends React.Component {
  render() {
    return <h1>Welcome to React!</h1>;
  }
}
```

3. **Props**:

   o **Props** (short for properties) are the mechanism by which data is passed from a parent component to a child component. Props are read-only, meaning that the child component cannot modify the props it receives; it can only use them to render UI.

   o Example of using props:

   jsx

```
function Greeting(props) {
  return <h1>Hello, {props.name}!</h1>;
}

// Passing 'name' prop from parent component
<Greeting name="Alice" />
```

   In this case, the Greeting component receives a name prop from its parent and uses it to render a personalized greeting.

State Management and Lifecycle Methods

React's **state management** and **lifecycle methods** are core concepts that allow you to build dynamic applications that respond to user interactions and other events.

1. **State**:
   - **State** is a JavaScript object that stores the data or properties that change over time in a React component. Unlike props, state is **mutable** and can be updated by the component itself using the setState() method (for class components) or the useState() hook (for functional components).

   Example (class component with state):

   jsx

   ```
   class Counter extends React.Component {
     constructor(props) {
       super(props);
       this.state = { count: 0 };
     }

     increment = () => {
       this.setState({ count: this.state.count + 1 });
     };

     render() {
       return (
   ```

```
<div>
  <h1>Count: {this.state.count}</h1>
  <button onClick={this.increment}>Increment</button>
</div>
    );
  }
}
```

Example (functional component with useState):

jsx

```
function Counter() {
  const [count, setCount] = useState(0);

  const increment = () => setCount(count + 1);

  return (
    <div>
      <h1>Count: {count}</h1>
      <button onClick={increment}>Increment</button>
    </div>
  );
}
```

2. **Lifecycle Methods**:

   o **Lifecycle methods** are special methods in class components that allow you to hook into different stages of the component's lifecycle, such as when it's created, updated, or destroyed. Common lifecycle methods include:

- **componentDidMount()**: Called once the component is mounted in the DOM.
- **componentDidUpdate()**: Called after the component updates due to a state or prop change.
- **componentWillUnmount()**: Called just before the component is removed from the DOM.

Example:

jsx

```
class MyComponent extends React.Component {
 componentDidMount() {
  console.log('Component mounted!');
 }

 render() {
  return <h1>Welcome!</h1>;
 }
}
```

In **functional components**, React introduced the useEffect hook to handle side effects like data fetching, subscriptions, or manual DOM manipulation.

jsx

```jsx
import { useEffect } from 'react';

function MyComponent() {
  useEffect(() => {
    console.log('Component mounted!');
  }, []);

  return <h1>Welcome!</h1>;
}
```

Real-World Example: Creating a React-Based Weather App

Now, let's create a **weather app** using React. This app will display the current weather for a given city by fetching data from a weather API. Users can enter the city name, and the app will display the weather information dynamically.

Step   1:   Set   Up   the   App

First, initialize a new React app using **Create React App**.

bash

```bash
npx create-react-app weather-app
cd weather-app
npm start
```

Step 2: Building the Weather Component

Create a Weather component that will handle the fetching and displaying of the weather data.

jsx

```jsx
import React, { useState, useEffect } from 'react';

function Weather() {
  const [city, setCity] = useState('');
  const [weatherData, setWeatherData] = useState(null);
  const [error, setError] = useState(null);

  const fetchWeather = async () => {
    if (city) {
      try {
        const response = await fetch(`https://api.openweathermap.org/data/2.5/weather?q=${city}&appid=YOUR_API_KEY&units=metric`);
        const data = await response.json();
        if (data.cod === 200) {
          setWeatherData(data);
          setError(null);
        } else {
          setError('City not found');
          setWeatherData(null);
        }
      } catch (err) {
        setError('Failed to fetch weather data');
        setWeatherData(null);
      }
```

```
  }
};

useEffect(() => {
  if (city) fetchWeather();
}, [city]);

return (
  <div>
    <h1>Weather App</h1>
    <input
      type="text"
      value={city}
      onChange={(e) => setCity(e.target.value)}
      placeholder="Enter city name"
    />
    <button onClick={fetchWeather}>Get Weather</button>
    {error && <p>{error}</p>}
    {weatherData && (
      <div>
        <h2>{weatherData.name}</h2>
        <p>{weatherData.weather[0].description}</p>
        <p>{weatherData.main.temp}°C</p>
      </div>
    )}
  </div>
);
}

export default Weather;
```

Explanation:

- We use useState to store the city input, weather data, and any error messages.
- The fetchWeather function fetches data from the OpenWeather API, processes the response, and updates the state with the weather information or an error message.
- We use useEffect to trigger the fetchWeather function whenever the city state changes.
- The app displays an input field for entering the city, a button to trigger the fetch, and the weather data (or error message) once it's fetched.

Step 3: Display the Weather Component

Now, in the App.js file, render the Weather component:

jsx

```
import React from 'react';
import Weather from './Weather';

function App() {
 return (
  <div className="App">
   <Weather />
  </div>
 );
}
```

export default App;

Summary

In this chapter, we introduced **React** and explored its core concepts, such as **JSX syntax**, **components**, **props**, **state management**, and **lifecycle methods**. We also highlighted the benefits of React's **component-based architecture** and **virtual DOM**.

By building a **weather app** in React, we demonstrated how to use **state** and **event handling** to create dynamic, interactive UIs. The example showed how to fetch data from an external API and display it using React's **component lifecycle** and **hooks**.

With this foundational knowledge, you can start building more complex and interactive applications using React, leveraging its powerful features to create seamless, real-time user experiences.

Chapter 8: Going Further with React

As you continue your journey with React, you'll encounter more advanced tools and techniques that help you manage routing, state, and side effects effectively in larger applications. In this chapter, we will dive deeper into some of these advanced concepts, including **React Router** for navigation, **React Hooks** like useState and useEffect, and state management solutions like **Context API** and **Redux**.

We'll also apply these concepts in a **real-world example** of building a simple **blog** application with React.

React Router for Navigation

In single-page applications (SPAs), navigation between different views or pages is handled without full page reloads. This is where **React Router** comes in. React Router is a standard library used for adding **client-side routing** to React applications.

1. **What is React Router?**
   React Router allows you to declaratively manage the navigation of your application, enabling users to navigate between different views (or pages) of your app without a page reload.

2. **Installing React Router**: To get started, you first need to install React Router:

bash

npm install react-router-dom

3. **Basic Usage**: React Router consists of several components that help manage routes:

- o <BrowserRouter>: A wrapper that enables routing functionality for your app.
- o <Route>: Defines a route that renders a component when the URL matches.
- o <Link>: Used to create navigation links that change the URL without a page reload.

Example of a simple routing setup:

jsx

```
import React from 'react';
import { BrowserRouter as Router, Route, Link } from 'react-router-dom';

function Home() {
  return <h2>Home Page</h2>;
}

function About() {
  return <h2>About Page</h2>;
}
```

```
function App() {
  return (
    <Router>
      <nav>
        <ul>
          <li>
            <Link to="/">Home</Link>
          </li>
          <li>
            <Link to="/about">About</Link>
          </li>
        </ul>
      </nav>
      <Route path="/" exact component={Home} />
      <Route path="/about" component={About} />
    </Router>
  );
}

export default App;
```

- o **<Link>** replaces traditional anchor tags (<a>) to navigate between pages without reloading.
- o **<Route>** defines what component should render when a specific path is matched.

4. **Nested Routes**: React Router allows you to define **nested routes**. For example:

jsx

```
function Blog() {
  return (
   <div>
    <h2>Blog</h2>
    <Route path="/blog/:id" component={BlogPost} />
   </div>
  );
}
```

5. **Redirecting Users**: You can also programmatically redirect users using the <Redirect> component or by using useHistory() or useNavigate() hooks in functional components.

React Hooks: useState, useEffect, and More

React introduced **hooks** in version 16.8 to allow functional components to use features like state and lifecycle methods, which were previously only available in class components. Let's look at two essential hooks: useState and useEffect.

1. **useState Hook**: The useState hook is used to manage state in functional components. It returns an array with two values:
   - The current state value.
   - A function to update the state.

   Example:

jsx

```jsx
import React, { useState } from 'react';

function Counter() {
  const [count, setCount] = useState(0);

  const increment = () => setCount(count + 1);

  return (
    <div>
      <p>Count: {count}</p>
      <button onClick={increment}>Increment</button>
    </div>
  );
}

export default Counter;
```

2. **useEffect Hook**: The useEffect hook is used to perform side effects in functional components. It is analogous to the lifecycle methods componentDidMount, componentDidUpdate, and componentWillUnmount in class components.

Example:

jsx

```jsx
import React, { useState, useEffect } from 'react';
```

```
function FetchData() {
  const [data, setData] = useState([]);

  useEffect(() => {
    fetch('https://api.example.com/data')
      .then(response => response.json())
      .then(data => setData(data));
  }, []);   // Empty array ensures the effect runs only once after the
component mounts

  return (
    <div>
      <ul>
        {data.map(item => (
          <li key={item.id}>{item.name}</li>
        ))}
      </ul>
    </div>
  );
}

export default FetchData;
```

The second argument of useEffect is the **dependency array**, which tells React when to run the effect (e.g., on component mount, on state or prop changes, or when certain dependencies change).

3. **Other Useful Hooks**:

- o useContext: Access global state provided by the Context API.
- o useReducer: An alternative to useState for managing more complex state logic.
- o useRef: A hook for accessing DOM elements and persisting values between renders.

Managing State with Context API or Redux

1. **Context API**: The **Context API** is a simpler, built-in solution for state management in React. It allows you to share state across components without passing props down manually at every level.

Example:

jsx

import React, { createContext, useState, useContext } from 'react';

const MyContext = createContext();

function ParentComponent() {
  const [value, setValue] = useState('Hello, World!');
  return (
    <MyContext.Provider value={{ value, setValue }}>
    <ChildComponent />

```
   </MyContext.Provider>
  );
 }


function ChildComponent() {
  const { value, setValue } = useContext(MyContext);
  return (
   <div>
    <p>{value}</p>
    <button  onClick={()  =>  setValue('New  Value')}>Change
Value</button>
   </div>
  );
 }
```

2. **Redux**: **Redux** is a state management library that works well with React, especially in large applications. It provides a centralized store for managing state and uses **actions** and **reducers** to update state.

   o **Actions**: Plain JavaScript objects that describe state changes.

   o **Reducers**: Functions that specify how the application's state changes in response to actions.

Example:

jsx

// Action

```
const increment = () => ({ type: 'INCREMENT' });

// Reducer
function counterReducer(state = { count: 0 }, action) {
  switch (action.type) {
    case 'INCREMENT':
      return { count: state.count + 1 };
    default:
      return state;
  }
}
```

To use Redux, you'll need to **connect** your components to the store using connect() or the **useDispatch** and **useSelector** hooks.

Real-World Example: Building a Blog with React

Now let's combine the concepts we've learned so far by building a simple **blog** application in React. This app will fetch a list of blog posts from an API and display them in a list. Users can click on a post to see more details.

Step 1: Setting Up the App

First, create a new React app:

bash

npx create-react-app blog-app

```
cd blog-app
npm start
```

Step 2: Fetching and Displaying Blog Posts

We'll start by creating a BlogList component that fetches and displays a list of blog posts.

jsx

```jsx
import React, { useState, useEffect } from 'react';

function BlogList() {
  const [posts, setPosts] = useState([]);

  useEffect(() => {
    fetch('https://jsonplaceholder.typicode.com/posts')
      .then(response => response.json())
      .then(data => setPosts(data));
  }, []);

  return (
    <div>
      <h1>Blog Posts</h1>
      <ul>
        {posts.map(post => (
          <li key={post.id}>
            <h2>{post.title}</h2>
            <p>{post.body}</p>
          </li>
        ))}
```

```
    </ul>
  </div>
 );
}
```

export default BlogList;

Step 3: Creating a Single Post View

Now, let's add a route for viewing individual blog posts using React Router. We'll create a BlogPost component to display the details of a single post.

jsx

```
import React, { useState, useEffect } from 'react';
import { useParams } from 'react-router-dom';

function BlogPost() {
  const { id } = useParams();
  const [post, setPost] = useState(null);

  useEffect(() => {
    fetch(`https://jsonplaceholder.typicode.com/posts/${id}`)
      .then(response => response.json())
      .then(data => setPost(data));
  }, [id]);

  if (!post) return <p>Loading...</p>;

  return (
```

```
<div>
  <h1>{post.title}</h1>
  <p>{post.body}</p>
</div>
 );
}
```

export default BlogPost;

Step 4: Adding Routes with React Router

In App.js, we'll use React Router to handle navigation between the blog list and individual post views.

jsx

```
import React from 'react';
import { BrowserRouter as Router, Route, Switch } from 'react-router-dom';
import BlogList from './BlogList';
import BlogPost from './BlogPost';

function App() {
  return (
    <Router>
      <Switch>
        <Route path="/" exact component={BlogList} />
        <Route path="/post/:id" component={BlogPost} />
      </Switch>
    </Router>
  );
}
```

export default App;

Explanation:

- BlogList fetches and displays the list of posts.
- BlogPost fetches and displays the details of a single post when clicked.
- React Router handles navigation between the list and the detailed post views.

Summary

In this chapter, we explored **advanced React concepts**, including **React Router** for navigation, **React Hooks** for managing state and side effects, and state management with the **Context API** and **Redux**. We also built a **real-world blog application** that demonstrates these concepts in action.

By mastering these advanced topics, you can build more sophisticated, scalable, and maintainable applications with React, enhancing your ability to create interactive and dynamic web applications. React's ecosystem, with tools like React Router and Redux, empowers developers to handle routing, state, and effects in a clean and efficient manner.

Chapter 9: Introduction to Front-End Frameworks: Angular

Angular is a comprehensive front-end framework developed and maintained by **Google**. It is used for building dynamic, single-page web applications (SPAs) by providing a structured, efficient way to develop client-side applications with powerful tools, such as two-way data binding, dependency injection, and a modular architecture. Angular's comprehensive approach makes it suitable for building complex, enterprise-level applications.

In this chapter, we will explore **what Angular is**, the **key Angular concepts** such as **components**, **modules**, **services**, and **directives**, as well as important features like **data binding** and **dependency injection**. We'll also walk through a **real-world example** of creating a **dynamic form** with Angular.

What is Angular and Why Use It?

Angular is a **TypeScript-based framework** that provides everything needed to build a modern web application. Unlike simpler libraries like React, which primarily focuses on building user interfaces, Angular is a full-fledged framework that includes solutions for:

1. **Routing**: For navigation between views without page reloads.

2. **Form management**: For handling complex forms and form validation.

3. **HTTP client**: For making HTTP requests to APIs.

4. **Testing utilities**: For unit and integration testing your application.

5. **Built-in development tools**: Such as Angular CLI (Command Line Interface), which helps with scaffolding, building, and serving the application.

Why use Angular?

- **Modular Structure**: Angular uses **modules** to organize an application, which helps in scaling projects effectively.

- **Two-Way Data Binding**: Angular's two-way data binding allows for automatic synchronization between the model (data) and the view (UI), making it easier to handle user inputs and display real-time updates.

- **Dependency Injection (DI)**: Angular's DI system allows for better code organization and testing by managing dependencies in a centralized manner.

- **Declarative Templates**: Angular's templates use HTML with embedded Angular directives to declaratively define how the UI should behave.

Angular is best suited for large-scale applications with complex features that require tools like routing, state management, and modularity right out of the box.

Key Angular Concepts: Components, Modules, Services, and Directives

Angular's architecture revolves around several key concepts that help structure applications in a maintainable and scalable way.

1. **Components**:
   - Components are the core building blocks of Angular applications. They define the **view** (UI) and behavior of a part of the application.
   - A component consists of three main parts:
     - **Template**: Defines the HTML layout.
     - **Class**: Contains the component's logic (e.g., methods and properties).
     - **Metadata**: Defined by the @Component decorator, this provides additional configuration such as the template and styles.

   Example of a simple component:

   typescript

   ```
   import { Component } from '@angular/core';
   ```

```typescript
@Component({
  selector: 'app-hello-world',
  template: '<h1>Hello, World!</h1>',
})
export class HelloWorldComponent {}
```

2. **Modules**:

   o Angular apps are structured as **modules**, which are containers for components, services, and other Angular features. The root module (AppModule) is used to bootstrap the application.

   o **NgModule** is an important decorator that groups related functionality together.

   Example of a module:

   typescript

```typescript
import { NgModule } from '@angular/core';
import { BrowserModule } from '@angular/platform-browser';
import { HelloWorldComponent } from './hello-world.component';

@NgModule({
  declarations: [HelloWorldComponent],
  imports: [BrowserModule],
  bootstrap: [HelloWorldComponent]
})
export class AppModule {}
```

3. **Services**:

   o **Services** are used to share data and business logic across components. They are typically used to interact with APIs, handle data, and perform operations.

   o Services are injected into components using Angular's **dependency injection** system, ensuring that data and functionality are available in the right places.

   Example of a service:

   typescript

   ```
   import { Injectable } from '@angular/core';

   @Injectable({
     providedIn: 'root'
   })
   export class DataService {
     getData() {
       return 'Some data from the service';
     }
   }
   ```

4. **Directives**:

   o Directives are special markers in Angular templates that modify the DOM or behavior of elements. They can either be **structural** (e.g., *ngFor, *ngIf) or **attribute-based** (e.g., ngClass, ngStyle).

Example of using a structural directive:

html

<div *ngFor="let item of items">{{ item }}</div>

Data Binding and Dependency Injection in Angular

1. **Data Binding**:
   - o Angular provides several types of **data binding** that allow you to synchronize data between the model (component) and the view (HTML template):
     - **Interpolation**: {{ data }} − Displays component data inside the HTML.
     - **Property Binding**: [property]="data" − Binds component data to an element's property.
     - **Event Binding**: (event)="method()" − Triggers a method when an event occurs.
     - **Two-Way Binding**: [(ngModel)]="data" − Binds both input values and component data, allowing two-way communication.

Example of two-way binding:

html

```
<input [(ngModel)]="name" />
<p>Hello, {{ name }}!</p>
```

2. **Dependency Injection**:

   o **Dependency injection** (DI) is a design pattern used in Angular to manage the services and dependencies that your components need.

   o Angular's DI system allows you to define services that can be injected into components, making it easier to manage dependencies and reduce code duplication.

   o Angular injects services through the constructor of the component or service that needs them.

Example of using DI:

typescript

```
import { Component } from '@angular/core';
import { DataService } from './data.service';

@Component({
  selector: 'app-root',
  template: `<p>{{ data }}</p>`
})
export class AppComponent {
  data: string;
```

```
constructor(private dataService: DataService) {
  this.data = this.dataService.getData();
}
}
```

Real-World Example: Creating a Dynamic Form with Angular

Let's apply the concepts we've learned by building a **dynamic form** with Angular. This form will allow users to input data and dynamically add more fields as needed.

Step 1: Setting Up the Angular App

Create a new Angular project using the Angular CLI:

bash

```
ng new dynamic-form-app
cd dynamic-form-app
ng serve
```

Step 2: Building the Form Component

Create a form component that will handle user input and allow adding dynamic fields.

bash

```
ng generate component dynamic-form
```

Edit the dynamic-form.component.ts file to create the form and handle adding new fields.

typescript

```typescript
import { Component } from '@angular/core';

@Component({
  selector: 'app-dynamic-form',
  templateUrl: './dynamic-form.component.html',
  styleUrls: ['./dynamic-form.component.css']
})
export class DynamicFormComponent {
  fields: string[] = ["];

  addField() {
    this.fields.push(");
  }

  removeField(index: number) {
    this.fields.splice(index, 1);
  }
}
```

Step 3: Creating the Form Template

Now, edit the dynamic-form.component.html to display the form and handle adding/removing fields.

html

```
<div>
 <form>
  <div *ngFor="let field of fields; let i = index">
   <label for="field{{ i }}">Field {{ i + 1 }}:</label>
   <input id="field{{ i }}" [(ngModel)]="fields[i]" name="field{{ i }}"
type="text">
   <button type="button" (click)="removeField(i)">Remove</button>
  </div>
  <button type="button" (click)="addField()">Add Field</button>
 </form>
</div>
```

Step 4: Styling the Form

You can add some simple styling for the form to make it more visually appealing. Edit the dynamic-form.component.css file:

css

```css
form {
  margin: 20px;
}

label {
  margin-right: 10px;
}

button {
  margin: 5px;
}
```

Summary

In this chapter, we introduced **Angular** and explored key concepts such as **components**, **modules**, **services**, and **directives**. We also examined important features like **data binding** and **dependency injection** that make Angular a powerful framework for building complex, scalable web applications.

We demonstrated how to create a **dynamic form** with Angular, allowing users to add and remove form fields dynamically. This example highlights how Angular's features, such as two-way data binding and event handling, can be used to build interactive user interfaces.

With these tools and concepts, you are well-equipped to start building sophisticated, maintainable applications with Angular.

Chapter 10: Advanced Angular Concepts

In this chapter, we will dive into some advanced concepts in Angular that are essential for building large-scale, interactive, and efficient web applications. These concepts include **Angular Routing** for navigation, **Forms and Validation** for handling user input, and **RxJS and Observables** for managing asynchronous data. Finally, we will walk through a **real-world example** of creating a **user authentication system** with Angular.

Angular Routing for Navigation

Routing in Angular allows you to navigate between views or components without a full page reload. It is an essential feature in single-page applications (SPAs), where the app needs to update the content dynamically based on the URL.

1. **Setting Up Angular Routing**:
    - To enable routing in an Angular application, you must first import the **RouterModule** into your app module and define the routes that map to specific components.
    - You can then use Angular's <router-outlet> directive in your template to render the routed component.

2. **Installing and Configuring Routing**: If you didn't select routing when creating the Angular project, you can add routing manually. Here's how you can set it up:

bash

ng generate module app-routing --flat --module=app

In the app-routing.module.ts file, define your routes:

typescript

```
import { NgModule } from '@angular/core';
import { RouterModule, Routes } from '@angular/router';
import { HomeComponent } from './home/home.component';
import { AboutComponent } from './about/about.component';

const routes: Routes = [
  { path: '', component: HomeComponent },
  { path: 'about', component: AboutComponent }
];

@NgModule({
  imports: [RouterModule.forRoot(routes)],
  exports: [RouterModule]
})
export class AppRoutingModule { }
```

3. **Navigation with Angular Router**:

   o Use the <router-outlet> directive in your app.component.html to display routed components.

o Use routerLink to define clickable links that allow navigation between views:

html

```html
<nav>
  <a routerLink="/">Home</a>
  <a routerLink="/about">About</a>
</nav>
<router-outlet></router-outlet>
```

4. **Navigating Programmatically**: You can also navigate programmatically using Angular's **Router** service:

typescript

```typescript
import { Router } from '@angular/router';

constructor(private router: Router) {}

navigateToAbout() {
  this.router.navigate(['/about']);
}
```

5. **Route Parameters**: You can pass parameters in the URL and access them in the target component:

typescript

```typescript
const routes: Routes = [
```

```
{ path: 'profile/:id', component: ProfileComponent }
];
```

In the ProfileComponent, you can retrieve the parameter using Angular's **ActivatedRoute**:

typescript

```
import { ActivatedRoute } from '@angular/router';

constructor(private route: ActivatedRoute) {
  this.route.params.subscribe(params => {
    console.log(params['id']);
  });
}
```

Forms and Validation in Angular

Forms are crucial in web applications for collecting user input, and Angular provides robust tools for handling both **template-driven forms** and **reactive forms**. Angular also includes built-in validation capabilities to ensure that the data entered by users is valid before submission.

1. **Template-Driven Forms**:
    o   Template-driven forms rely on Angular's directives such as ngModel to bind form controls to the model.

o You can use Angular's built-in validation directives like required, minlength, and pattern for basic form validation.

Example:

html

```
<form #form="ngForm" (ngSubmit)="onSubmit(form)">
 <input    type="text"    name="username"    ngModel    required
minlength="3" #username="ngModel">
 <div *ngIf="username.invalid && username.touched">
  <small    *ngIf="username.errors.required">Username    is
required.</small>
  <small *ngIf="username.errors.minlength">Username must be at
least 3 characters long.</small>
 </div>
 <button type="submit" [disabled]="form.invalid">Submit</button>
</form>
```

2. **Reactive Forms**:

   o Reactive forms give you more control over the form's structure and validation. You define form controls in your component class using Angular's FormBuilder and FormGroup services.

   o Reactive forms allow you to easily manage complex form validation and dynamic form controls.

Example:

typescript

```
import { Component } from '@angular/core';
import { FormBuilder, FormGroup, Validators } from '@angular/forms';

@Component({
  selector: 'app-login',
  templateUrl: './login.component.html'
})
export class LoginComponent {
  loginForm: FormGroup;

  constructor(private fb: FormBuilder) {
    this.loginForm = this.fb.group({
      username: ['', [Validators.required, Validators.minLength(3)]],
      password: ['', Validators.required]
    });
  }

  onSubmit() {
    if (this.loginForm.valid) {
      console.log(this.loginForm.value);
    }
  }
}
```

3. **Custom Validation**:
   - o You can create custom validators to perform more complex checks on form inputs.
   - o Example of a custom validator:

typescript

```typescript
import { AbstractControl } from '@angular/forms';

export function forbiddenNameValidator(control: AbstractControl) {
  if (control.value === 'admin') {
    return { 'forbiddenName': true };
  }
  return null;
}
```

RxJS and Observables

RxJS (Reactive Extensions for JavaScript) is a powerful library for handling asynchronous operations and events using **Observables**. It is heavily integrated into Angular for managing HTTP requests, form values, routing events, and more.

1. **Observables**:
   - An **Observable** is a stream of data that can be observed and subscribed to. Observables are used to handle asynchronous data flows such as HTTP responses, user inputs, or events.
   - In Angular, many services (such as HttpClient) return Observables to allow the handling of asynchronous data.

   Example of creating an Observable:

```typescript
import { Observable } from 'rxjs';

const numbers = new Observable<number>(observer => {
  observer.next(1);
  observer.next(2);
  observer.complete();
});

numbers.subscribe(value => console.log(value));
```

2. **Operators**:

   - RxJS provides a wide range of **operators** (such as map, filter, mergeMap, catchError) that allow you to transform, filter, and combine observables.
   - Example of using the map operator:

```typescript
import { Observable } from 'rxjs';
import { map } from 'rxjs/operators';

this.httpClient.get('/api/data').pipe(
  map(response => response['data'])
).subscribe(data => console.log(data));
```

3. **Subject**:

o A **Subject** is a special type of Observable that allows you to multicast to multiple observers. Subjects are useful for event handling and for implementing services like the **EventEmitter**.

Example:

typescript

```
import { Subject } from 'rxjs';

const subject = new Subject<number>();

subject.subscribe(value => console.log(value));
subject.next(1);
subject.next(2);
```

Real-World Example: Building a User Authentication System with Angular

Let's put these advanced Angular concepts into practice by building a simple **user authentication system**. This system will include a login form, error handling, and a basic authentication service to manage user sessions.

Step 1: Setting Up the Authentication Service

Create a service that will handle login, authentication, and storing the user's session.

bash

ng generate service auth

In auth.service.ts:

typescript

```
import { Injectable } from '@angular/core';
import { BehaviorSubject } from 'rxjs';

@Injectable({
  providedIn: 'root'
})
export class AuthService {
  private loggedIn = new BehaviorSubject<boolean>(false);

  login(username: string, password: string) {
    if (username === 'user' && password === 'password') {
      this.loggedIn.next(true);
    } else {
      this.loggedIn.next(false);
    }
  }

  get isLoggedIn() {
    return this.loggedIn.asObservable();
  }
}
```

Step 2: Creating the Login Component

Create a login form that allows users to enter their credentials and authenticate.

bash

ng generate component login

In login.component.ts:

typescript

```typescript
import { Component } from '@angular/core';
import { AuthService } from './auth.service';

@Component({
  selector: 'app-login',
  templateUrl: './login.component.html'
})
export class LoginComponent {
  username: string = '';
  password: string = '';
  errorMessage: string = '';

  constructor(private authService: AuthService) {}

  login() {
    this.authService.login(this.username, this.password);
    this.authService.isLoggedIn.subscribe(loggedIn => {
      if (!loggedIn) {
        this.errorMessage = 'Invalid username or password';
      } else {
```

```
    // Navigate to dashboard
  }
  });
 }
}
```

In login.component.html:

html

```
<form (ngSubmit)="login()">
  <label for="username">Username:</label>
  <input type="text" [(ngModel)]="username" name="username" required>
  <label for="password">Password:</label>
  <input type="password" [(ngModel)]="password" name="password" required>
  <button type="submit">Login</button>
</form>
<p *ngIf="errorMessage">{{ errorMessage }}</p>
```

Summary

In this chapter, we covered advanced Angular concepts essential for building robust, scalable applications:

1. **Angular Routing**: Enables navigation between views without a page reload, using routes, routerLink, and router-outlet.
2. **Forms and Validation**: Discussed how to create both **template-driven** and **reactive forms** with built-in validation, as well as custom validation techniques.

3. **RxJS and Observables**: Introduced the core concepts of RxJS for managing asynchronous data flows, including Observables, operators, and Subjects.

4. **Real-World Example**: We built a basic **user authentication system** using Angular's routing, forms, and services, demonstrating the practical application of these advanced concepts.

By mastering these advanced topics, you can build more interactive, maintainable, and efficient Angular applications that are well-suited to handle real-world use cases.

Chapter 11: Introduction to Front-End Frameworks: Vue.js

Vue.js is a progressive **JavaScript framework** used for building **user interfaces** and **single-page applications (SPAs)**. Unlike other frameworks, Vue.js is designed to be incrementally adoptable. This means that you can start with simple, small pieces of functionality and gradually scale your application as needed. Its simplicity, flexibility, and performance make it an excellent choice for both beginners and experienced developers.

In this chapter, we will explore **what Vue.js is** and why you should use it, dive into **Vue.js fundamentals** like the **Vue instance**, **directives**, and **components**, and learn how to implement **two-way data binding**. We will also build a **task manager app** using Vue.js as a real-world example.

What is Vue.js and Why Use It?

Vue.js is an open-source **JavaScript framework** created by **Evan You**. It is used for building interactive user interfaces and SPAs. Vue's core library focuses solely on the **view layer**, making it easy to integrate with other libraries or existing projects. It is **flexible**, allowing you to scale from simple interactive web elements to full-fledged, complex single-page applications.

Why use Vue.js?

1. **Ease of Learning**:
   - o Vue.js has a gentle learning curve and a simple syntax. If you're familiar with HTML, CSS, and JavaScript, you can quickly get started with Vue without much overhead.
   - o Vue's detailed and well-structured documentation also makes learning Vue easy for both beginners and experienced developers.

2. **Flexibility and Integration**:
   - o Vue can be used for building simple, small features or large-scale, complex applications. It integrates easily with other libraries or existing web applications.
   - o For complex applications, Vue provides an **ecosystem** of tools like **Vue Router** for navigation, **Vuex** for state management, and **Vue CLI** for scaffolding projects.

3. **Performance**:
   - o Vue.js is highly optimized for performance. It uses an **efficient virtual DOM** and can re-render only the parts of the DOM that need to be updated, ensuring fast updates even in large applications.

4. **Two-Way Data Binding**:

○ Vue makes it easy to create dynamic, real-time applications by providing two-way data binding. This feature ensures that any changes in the data model are immediately reflected in the view, and any changes in the view are instantly reflected in the data model.

5. **Vue's Ecosystem**:

○ Vue offers a comprehensive ecosystem for building advanced applications. The **Vue Router** handles routing, **Vuex** manages state, and tools like **Vue CLI** simplify development.

Vue.js Fundamentals: Vue Instance, Directives, and Components

1. **Vue Instance**:

○ The **Vue instance** is the root of every Vue.js application. It is the object that binds the application's data to the DOM and allows you to use Vue's reactivity system.

○ A basic Vue instance is created using the new Vue() syntax, where you pass in an options object that defines data, methods, and the template.

Example:

javascript

```javascript
new Vue({
  el: '#app',
  data: {
    message: 'Hello, Vue!'
  }
});
```

- ○ Here, el specifies the DOM element that Vue should control, and data holds the application's state.

2. **Vue Directives**:

- ○ **Directives** are special attributes in Vue.js that allow you to apply special behavior to DOM elements.
- ○ Common directives include:
  - ▪ **v-bind**: Dynamically binds an attribute to an expression.
  - ▪ **v-model**: Creates two-way data binding between form input elements and data.
  - ▪ **v-if / v-else**: Conditionally renders elements.
  - ▪ **v-for**: Loops through an array and renders a list of items.

Example of v-bind:

html

```html
<img v-bind:src="imageUrl" alt="Vue logo">
```

Example of v-for:

html

```
<ul>
 <li v-for="task in tasks" :key="task.id">{{ task.name }}</li>
</ul>
```

3. **Vue Components**:

   o **Components** are reusable building blocks in Vue. Each component has its own view (template), logic (data, methods), and style (CSS).

   o You define a component using Vue.component() or as an object within a Vue instance or component options.

Example of a simple component:

javascript

```
Vue.component('task-item', {
  props: ['task'],
  template: '<li>{{ task.name }}</li>'
});
```

Components can be nested inside other components to create complex UIs, making them perfect for building scalable, maintainable applications.

Two-Way Data Binding with Vue

One of the standout features of Vue.js is its **two-way data binding**. With two-way binding, changes to the model are automatically reflected in the view, and changes in the view are immediately reflected in the model.

Vue uses the v-model directive to create two-way data binding between form elements (such as input fields, checkboxes, and select options) and the component's data.

Example of two-way binding with v-model:

html

```
<div id="app">
  <input v-model="message" placeholder="Edit me">
  <p>Message: {{ message }}</p>
</div>

<script>
  new Vue({
    el: '#app',
    data: {
      message: "
    }
  });
</script>
```

- In this example, when you type in the input field, the message data property is updated automatically, and the paragraph reflects the change in real time.

Real-World Example: Building a Task Manager App with Vue.js

Now that we understand the core concepts of Vue.js, let's build a simple **task manager app** using Vue. This app will allow users to add tasks, display a list of tasks, and delete tasks.

Step 1: Setting Up the Vue App

First, create a basic HTML structure and include Vue.js in the <script> tag:

html

```
<!DOCTYPE html>
<html lang="en">
<head>
  <meta charset="UTF-8">
  <meta name="viewport" content="width=device-width, initial-scale=1.0">
  <title>Vue Task Manager</title>
</head>
<body>
  <div id="app">
    <h1>Task Manager</h1>
    <input v-model="newTask" placeholder="Enter a task" @keyup.enter="addTask">
```

```
<ul>
  <li v-for="(task, index) in tasks" :key="task.id">
    {{ task.name }} <button @click="removeTask(index)">Delete</button>
  </li>
</ul>
</div>

<script src="https://cdn.jsdelivr.net/npm/vue@2.6.14/dist/vue.js"></script>
<script>
  new Vue({
    el: '#app',
    data: {
      newTask: ",
      tasks: []
    },
    methods: {
      addTask() {
        if (this.newTask.trim() !== ") {
          this.tasks.push({ id: Date.now(), name: this.newTask });
          this.newTask = "; // Clear input field
        }
      },
      removeTask(index) {
        this.tasks.splice(index, 1);
      }
    }
  });
</script>
</body>
</html>
```

Step 2: Explanation

1. **Data**:
   - o newTask: Stores the value entered by the user in the input field.
   - o tasks: An array of task objects, where each object has an id and name.

2. **Two-Way Data Binding**:
   - o We use the v-model directive to bind the newTask data property to the input field. Any changes made to the input field will automatically update the newTask property.

3. **Methods**:
   - o addTask(): This method adds a new task to the tasks array when the user presses **Enter**. It uses the Date.now() function to generate a unique id for each task.
   - o removeTask(index): This method removes a task from the list by finding its index and using splice().

4. **Rendering**:
   - o The v-for directive is used to loop through the tasks array and display each task in an unordered list.
   - o The @click directive is used to call the removeTask() method when the "Delete" button is clicked.

Summary

In this chapter, we explored **Vue.js**, a powerful yet simple JavaScript framework for building dynamic user interfaces. We covered key Vue.js concepts like the **Vue instance**, **directives**, and **components**. We also discussed how **two-way data binding** works in Vue using v-model and created a simple **task manager app** that demonstrates these concepts in action.

Vue.js is a flexible, performance-oriented framework that allows developers to build interactive applications with minimal effort. By leveraging its core features, such as components and two-way data binding, you can quickly create dynamic, scalable web applications.

Chapter 12: Going Further with Vue.js

In this chapter, we will dive deeper into some advanced features of Vue.js, such as **Vue Router** for navigation, **Vuex** for state management, and the power of **component-based architecture** in Vue applications. We'll also walk through a **real-world example** by building a **movie search app** that demonstrates how these advanced features work together to build interactive and scalable web applications.

Vue Router for Navigation

Vue Router is an official library for handling routing in Vue.js applications. It allows you to navigate between different views or components in a single-page application (SPA) without reloading the page, providing a smooth user experience.

1. **Setting Up Vue Router**: To use Vue Router, first install it in your project:

    bash

    npm install vue-router

2. **Configuring Vue Router**: After installing Vue Router, you need to configure it by defining your routes in a router.js or similar file.

javascript

```javascript
import Vue from 'vue';
import VueRouter from 'vue-router';
import Home from './components/Home.vue';
import MovieDetails from './components/MovieDetails.vue';

Vue.use(VueRouter);

const routes = [
  { path: '/', component: Home },
  { path: '/movie/:id', component: MovieDetails, props: true }
];

const router = new VueRouter({
  routes
});

export default router;
```

- o **path**: Defines the URL pattern.
- o **component**: Specifies which component should be rendered when the path is matched.
- o **props: true**: Allows route parameters (such as id) to be passed as props to the component.

3. **Using Vue Router in the App**: In the main.js file, import and use the router:

javascript

```
import Vue from 'vue';
import App from './App.vue';
import router from './router';

new Vue({
  render: h => h(App),
  router
}).$mount('#app');
```

4. **Navigating with Vue Router**: To navigate between views, you can use the router-link directive or programmatically use the this.$router object.

   o **router-link**: Used in the template to create links between pages.

   html

   ```html
   <router-link to="/">Home</router-link>
   <router-link :to="'/movie/' + movie.id">Details</router-link>
   ```

   o **Programmatic Navigation**:

   javascript

   ```javascript
   this.$router.push('/movie/123');
   ```

Vuex for State Management

In larger applications, managing state can become complex. **Vuex** is the official state management library for Vue.js. It helps centralize the state management in a single store, making it easier to manage and share state across components.

1. **Setting Up Vuex**: First, install Vuex in your Vue.js project:

   bash

   npm install vuex

2. **Creating a Vuex Store**: In Vuex, you define a store that contains the application's state, mutations, actions, and getters.

   javascript

   import Vue from 'vue';
   import Vuex from 'vuex';

   Vue.use(Vuex);

   const store = new Vuex.Store({
     state: {
       movies: []
     },
     mutations: {
       setMovies(state, movies) {
         state.movies = movies;

```
      }
    },
    actions: {
      fetchMovies({ commit }) {
        // Call API to fetch movies
        fetch('https://api.example.com/movies')
          .then(response => response.json())
          .then(data => {
            commit('setMovies', data);
          });
      }
    },
    getters: {
      allMovies(state) {
        return state.movies;
      }
    }
});
```

export default store;

- o **state**: The central place where all the application's data is stored.
- o **mutations**: Functions that modify the state.
- o **actions**: Functions that can dispatch mutations, often used for asynchronous operations (e.g., fetching data from an API).
- o **getters**: Functions that return computed values derived from the state.

3. **Using Vuex in Components**: To access the state, dispatch actions, or commit mutations, you use the **$store** object inside components.

javascript

```
export default {
  computed: {
    movies() {
      return this.$store.getters.allMovies;
    }
  },
  created() {
    this.$store.dispatch('fetchMovies');
  }
}
```

- **$store.dispatch()**: Calls an action.
- **$store.getters**: Retrieves the state from the Vuex store.

4. **Vuex and Components**: Vuex allows multiple components to access and modify the shared state without directly passing data between them.

Component-Based Architecture

Vue.js follows a **component-based architecture**, where the user interface is split into isolated, reusable components. Each component has its own logic, template, and style. Components can be used inside other components to create complex UIs while keeping the codebase clean and maintainable.

1. **Component Structure**: Vue components are defined using a simple structure:

vue

```
<template>
  <div class="component">
    <h1>{{ message }}</h1>
  </div>
</template>

<script>
export default {
  data() {
    return {
      message: 'Hello from Vue component!'
    };
  }
};
</script>

<style scoped>
.component {
  font-size: 20px;
  color: blue;
}
</style>
```

- o **<template>**: Contains the HTML structure.
- o **<script>**: Contains the component logic (data, methods, computed properties).
- o **<style scoped>**: Scoped styles that apply only to this component.

2. **Passing Data Between Components**:
    - o **Props**: Used to pass data from a parent component to a child component.
    - o **Events**: Used to send data or trigger actions from a child component to a parent component.

Real-World Example: Building a Movie Search App with Vue.js

Let's now combine these concepts to build a **movie search app** where users can search for movies and view details.

Step 1: Setting Up the App

We'll use **Vue Router**, **Vuex**, and components to build this app. First, create a new Vue project:

bash

```
vue create movie-search-app
cd movie-search-app
```

Install Vue Router and Vuex:

bash

npm install vue-router vuex

Step 2: Create Components

1. **SearchComponent.vue** – The component where users can search for movies.

2. **MovieList.vue** – Displays the list of movies fetched from an API.

3. **MovieDetails.vue** – Displays detailed information about a selected movie.

Example of SearchComponent.vue:

vue

```
<template>
 <div>
   <input v-model="query" @keyup.enter="searchMovies" placeholder="Search
for movies..." />
   <button @click="searchMovies">Search</button>
 </div>
</template>

<script>
export default {
 data() {
  return {
   query: "
  };
```

```
  },
  methods: {
   searchMovies() {
    this.$store.dispatch('fetchMovies', this.query);
   }
  }
};
</script>
```

Step 3: Set Up Vuex Store

In the store.js file, define actions and mutations to fetch and store movie data.

javascript

```
import Vue from 'vue';
import Vuex from 'vuex';

Vue.use(Vuex);

export default new Vuex.Store({
  state: {
   movies: [],
   selectedMovie: null
  },
  mutations: {
   setMovies(state, movies) {
    state.movies = movies;
   },
   setSelectedMovie(state, movie) {
```

```
    state.selectedMovie = movie;
  }
},
 actions: {
  fetchMovies({ commit }, query) {

fetch(`https://api.themoviedb.org/3/search/movie?query=${query}&api_key=Y
OUR_API_KEY`)
      .then(response => response.json())
      .then(data => commit('setMovies', data.results));
  }
},
 getters: {
  allMovies: state => state.movies
  }
});
```

Step 4: Set Up Vue Router

In router.js, configure routes for movie search and details.

javascript

```
import Vue from 'vue';
import VueRouter from 'vue-router';
import MovieList from './components/MovieList.vue';
import MovieDetails from './components/MovieDetails.vue';

Vue.use(VueRouter);

const routes = [
  { path: '/', component: MovieList },
```

```
  { path: '/movie/:id', component: MovieDetails, props: true }
];

const router = new VueRouter({
  routes
});

export default router;
```

Step 5: Displaying Movie List and Details

Example of MovieList.vue:

vue

```vue
<template>
  <div>
    <h1>Movie List</h1>
    <ul>
      <li v-for="movie in movies" :key="movie.id">
        <router-link :to="'/movie/' + movie.id">{{ movie.title }}</router-link>
      </li>
    </ul>
  </div>
</template>

<script>
export default {
  computed: {
    movies() {
      return this.$store.getters.allMovies;
    }
```

```
  }
};
</script>
```

Step 6: Running the App

Finally, start the app:

bash

npm run serve

Summary

In this chapter, we explored advanced **Vue.js** concepts such as **Vue Router** for navigation, **Vuex** for state management, and how to build applications using a **component-based architecture**. We also built a real-world **movie search app** that demonstrates how to use these concepts effectively:

1. **Vue Router** was used to handle navigation between movie search results and movie details pages.
2. **Vuex** was used to manage the state of the movies and allow easy access across components.
3. **Components** were used to create reusable units like the search bar, movie list, and movie details.

By mastering these advanced features of Vue.js, you'll be able to build scalable, maintainable, and feature-rich web applications.

Chapter 13: Introduction to Back-End Frameworks

When developing a web application, the back-end refers to the server-side portion of the application that handles data processing, storage, and communication with the client-side. A **back-end framework** is a collection of tools and libraries that simplify the development of server-side applications. It helps developers create APIs, handle requests, manage databases, and perform other critical tasks in building a web application.

In this chapter, we will explore what a **back-end framework** is, the key concepts associated with it such as **RESTful APIs** and **CRUD operations**, and why using a back-end framework is beneficial. We will also walk through a **real-world example** of setting up a simple **Node.js back-end server**.

What is a Back-End Framework?

A **back-end framework** is a pre-built collection of libraries and tools that provides the basic infrastructure for developing back-end services. These frameworks are designed to handle common tasks such as:

- Routing and managing HTTP requests.
- Connecting to databases and handling data persistence.

- Managing authentication and authorization.
- Handling server-side logic and business logic.
- Serving static assets and files.

Some of the most popular back-end frameworks include:

- **Node.js** (with frameworks like **Express.js**).
- **Ruby on Rails**.
- **Django** (Python).
- **Flask** (Python).
- **Laravel** (PHP).

These frameworks provide developers with the foundational tools needed to create secure, efficient, and scalable back-end applications.

Key Concepts: RESTful API, CRUD Operations

1. **RESTful API**: A **RESTful API** (Representational State Transfer) is a design architecture for networked applications that uses HTTP requests to retrieve and manipulate data. The core principles of a RESTful API include stateless communication, a uniform interface, and the use of standard HTTP methods (GET, POST, PUT, DELETE) to perform operations.

Key characteristics of a RESTful API:

- **Stateless**: Each request from the client must contain all the information the server needs to fulfill that request. The server does not store any session data between requests.
- **Client-Server Architecture**: The client (front-end) and server (back-end) are separate, and communication between them happens over HTTP.
- **Resource-Based**: In a RESTful API, each resource (such as a user, post, or comment) is identified by a URL. The resources can be manipulated using standard HTTP methods.

Example of a RESTful URL for a blog:

- **GET /posts** – Fetches a list of all posts.
- **GET /posts/{id}** – Fetches a specific post by ID.
- **POST /posts** – Creates a new post.
- **PUT /posts/{id}** – Updates a post by ID.
- **DELETE /posts/{id}** – Deletes a post by ID.

2. **CRUD Operations**: **CRUD** stands for **Create**, **Read**, **Update**, and **Delete** – the four basic operations you can perform on any resource in a database.
    - **Create**: Adds new data to the database (usually via POST).

- o **Read**: Retrieves data from the database (usually via GET).
- o **Update**: Modifies existing data in the database (usually via PUT or PATCH).
- o **Delete**: Removes data from the database (usually via DELETE).

For example, in a blog application, CRUD operations would involve creating new posts, reading and displaying them, updating posts, and deleting them from the database.

Why Use a Back-End Framework?

1. **Faster Development**: A back-end framework provides you with pre-built tools and components that handle common back-end tasks such as routing, database connections, and request handling. This reduces the amount of time and code you need to write, enabling you to focus on building features rather than dealing with infrastructure.

2. **Security**: Frameworks provide built-in security features such as input validation, data sanitation, and protection against common web vulnerabilities (like SQL injection and Cross-Site Scripting). By using a framework, you ensure that your application follows best practices for securing user data.

3. **Maintainability**: Frameworks enforce a consistent structure for your codebase, making it easier to maintain and extend over time. They also help developers adhere to software design patterns such as **MVC** (Model-View-Controller), which separates concerns and makes it easier to manage large codebases.

4. **Scalability**: Frameworks provide tools that allow your application to scale effectively. This includes things like request handling, load balancing, and performance optimization. Additionally, many frameworks are built to work well with cloud-based platforms, making them ideal for deploying scalable applications.

5. **Community and Support**: Back-end frameworks typically have large, active communities that contribute to improving the framework and provide support through forums, tutorials, and documentation. You also get access to open-source plugins and libraries that can extend the functionality of your application.

Real-World Example: Setting Up a Simple Node.js Back-End Server

Let's now walk through setting up a simple **Node.js** back-end server with **Express.js**, a popular back-end framework for building RESTful APIs.

Step 1: Setting Up the Project

Start by creating a new Node.js project:

bash

```
mkdir node-backend
cd node-backend
npm init -y  # Initialize a new Node.js project
```

Install **Express.js**:

bash

```
npm install express
```

Step 2: Setting Up the Server

Create a file called server.js and set up a simple Express server:

javascript

```
const express = require('express');
const app = express();
const port = 3000;


app.use(express.json()); // Middleware to parse JSON bodies


// Sample data (in a real app, this would come from a database)
let tasks = [
  { id: 1, name: 'Learn JavaScript' },
  { id: 2, name: 'Build a Node.js server' },
];
```

```
// CRUD Operations (RESTful API)

// Get all tasks
app.get('/tasks', (req, res) => {
  res.json(tasks);
});

// Get a task by ID
app.get('/tasks/:id', (req, res) => {
  const task = tasks.find(t => t.id === parseInt(req.params.id));
  if (!task) return res.status(404).send('Task not found');
  res.json(task);
});

// Create a new task
app.post('/tasks', (req, res) => {
  const task = { id: tasks.length + 1, name: req.body.name };
  tasks.push(task);
  res.status(201).json(task);
});

// Update a task
app.put('/tasks/:id', (req, res) => {
  const task = tasks.find(t => t.id === parseInt(req.params.id));
  if (!task) return res.status(404).send('Task not found');
  task.name = req.body.name;
  res.json(task);
});
```

```
// Delete a task
app.delete('/tasks/:id', (req, res) => {
  const taskIndex = tasks.findIndex(t => t.id === parseInt(req.params.id));
  if (taskIndex === -1) return res.status(404).send('Task not found');
  tasks.splice(taskIndex, 1);
  res.status(204).send();
});


// Start the server
app.listen(port, () => {
  console.log(`Server is running at http://localhost:${port}`);
});
```

Step 3: Running the Server

To run the server, use the following command:

bash

node server.js

The server will be running at http://localhost:3000, and you can make HTTP requests using a tool like **Postman** or **cURL**.

- **GET /tasks**: Retrieve all tasks.
- **GET /tasks/:id**: Retrieve a task by ID.
- **POST /tasks**: Create a new task.
- **PUT /tasks/:id**: Update a task.
- **DELETE /tasks/:id**: Delete a task.

Summary

In this chapter, we explored the concept of **back-end frameworks** and how they simplify the process of building server-side applications. We learned about key concepts such as **RESTful APIs** and **CRUD operations**, which are essential for building web services that interact with databases.

We also walked through a **real-world example** of setting up a simple **Node.js back-end server** using **Express.js**. This server allows users to perform CRUD operations on tasks, demonstrating how back-end frameworks can help us efficiently handle routing, data processing, and server management.

By using back-end frameworks like Express, developers can build secure, scalable, and maintainable back-end applications that integrate seamlessly with front-end frameworks and provide powerful APIs for modern web applications.

Chapter 14: Introduction to Node.js and Express

In this chapter, we will explore **Node.js** and **Express.js**, two essential technologies for building back-end applications with JavaScript. Node.js provides the runtime environment for executing JavaScript on the server-side, and Express.js is a minimal and flexible web application framework built on top of Node.js that simplifies routing, middleware management, and handling HTTP requests. We will also build a basic RESTful API with Express and walk through a **real-world example** of creating a **simple to-do API**.

What is Node.js and Why Use It?

Node.js is an open-source, **cross-platform runtime environment** that allows developers to execute JavaScript code on the server-side. Traditionally, JavaScript was only used in the browser for client-side scripting, but with Node.js, JavaScript can now be used to build server-side applications, APIs, and more.

Key Features of Node.js:

1. **Event-Driven and Non-Blocking I/O**:
   - Node.js uses an event-driven, non-blocking I/O model that makes it lightweight and efficient. This means that Node.js can handle multiple requests

concurrently without blocking, which is ideal for building scalable applications that need to handle many simultaneous connections.

2. **Single-Threaded**:
   o Unlike traditional multi-threaded environments, Node.js uses a **single-threaded event loop** to handle requests. While this may sound limiting, the non-blocking nature of Node.js ensures that it can handle many operations efficiently, even with a single thread.

3. **Fast and Lightweight**:
   o Node.js is built on **V8**, Google's high-performance JavaScript engine, which makes it very fast. This, combined with its asynchronous I/O model, allows Node.js to perform well in I/O-heavy tasks like handling HTTP requests and reading/writing to databases.

4. **Package Management with npm**:
   o Node.js has **npm** (Node Package Manager), which is a vast repository of open-source libraries and tools that you can easily install and use in your project. npm makes it easy to add packages such as databases, authentication modules, and other utilities.

Why Use Node.js?:

- **JavaScript Everywhere**: With Node.js, you can use JavaScript for both the client-side (in the browser) and the server-side (on the backend). This makes it easier to work with, especially in full-stack development.

- **Real-Time Applications**: Node.js is great for building real-time applications, such as chat applications, live notifications, or online gaming, where rapid communication between the server and clients is essential.

- **Scalability**: Node.js is particularly useful in building scalable applications that need to handle a large number of concurrent connections, such as APIs and microservices.

Introduction to Express.js

Express.js is a minimal, fast, and flexible web application framework for **Node.js**. It simplifies the process of building web servers, handling HTTP requests, managing routes, and serving static files. Express provides a set of tools to handle common web development tasks, such as routing, middleware support, and HTTP request/response handling, making it the de facto standard for building web APIs and back-end services in Node.js.

Key Features of Express.js:

1. **Routing**: Express provides a powerful routing system that lets you define routes for handling various HTTP methods like GET, POST, PUT, and DELETE.

2. **Middleware**: Middleware functions allow you to execute code during the request-response cycle. This is useful for tasks such as authentication, logging, validation, and error handling.

3. **Template Engines**: Express supports integration with template engines (such as Pug or EJS) for rendering dynamic views.

4. **Serving Static Files**: Express makes it easy to serve static files like images, CSS, and JavaScript.

5. **Error Handling**: Express provides built-in error handling that helps catch and process errors in a centralized manner.

Building a Basic RESTful API with Express

A **RESTful API** allows different systems to communicate over HTTP, typically using JSON to send and receive data. In this section, we'll build a simple RESTful API using **Express.js** that handles CRUD operations (Create, Read, Update, Delete).

Step 1: Setting Up the Project

First, initialize a new Node.js project:

bash

```bash
mkdir express-api
cd express-api
npm init -y  # Initialize a new Node.js project
```

Install Express.js:

bash

```bash
npm install express
```

Step 2: Setting Up the Express Server

Create a file called server.js and set up a basic Express server:

javascript

```javascript
const express = require('express');
const app = express();
const port = 3000;

app.use(express.json()); // Middleware to parse JSON bodies

// Basic GET route
app.get('/', (req, res) => {
  res.send('Hello, World!');
});

// Start the server
app.listen(port, () => {
  console.log(`Server is running at http://localhost:${port}`);
});
```

This basic server listens on port 3000 and responds with "Hello, World!" when the root URL is accessed.

Step 3: Creating RESTful Routes

Next, let's create some basic CRUD routes for managing to-do items. We'll simulate storing tasks in memory (for simplicity) rather than using a database.

javascript

```javascript
let tasks = [
  { id: 1, task: 'Learn Node.js' },
  { id: 2, task: 'Build RESTful API' },
];

// GET /tasks: Fetch all tasks
app.get('/tasks', (req, res) => {
 res.json(tasks);
});

// GET /tasks/:id: Fetch a specific task by ID
app.get('/tasks/:id', (req, res) => {
  const task = tasks.find(t => t.id === parseInt(req.params.id));
  if (!task) return res.status(404).send('Task not found');
  res.json(task);
});

// POST /tasks: Create a new task
app.post('/tasks', (req, res) => {
```

```
const task = { id: tasks.length + 1, task: req.body.task };
tasks.push(task);
res.status(201).json(task);
});

// PUT /tasks/:id: Update a task
app.put('/tasks/:id', (req, res) => {
  const task = tasks.find(t => t.id === parseInt(req.params.id));
  if (!task) return res.status(404).send('Task not found');
  task.task = req.body.task;
  res.json(task);
});

// DELETE /tasks/:id: Delete a task
app.delete('/tasks/:id', (req, res) => {
  const taskIndex = tasks.findIndex(t => t.id === parseInt(req.params.id));
  if (taskIndex === -1) return res.status(404).send('Task not found');
  tasks.splice(taskIndex, 1);
  res.status(204).send();
});
```

Here, we define routes for:

- **GET /tasks**: Retrieves all tasks.
- **GET /tasks/:id**: Retrieves a specific task by ID.
- **POST /tasks**: Creates a new task.
- **PUT /tasks/:id**: Updates an existing task by ID.
- **DELETE /tasks/:id**: Deletes a task by ID.

Real-World Example: Creating a Simple To-Do API with Node.js and Express

Now, let's build a simple **To-Do API** using **Node.js** and **Express**.

Step 1: Set Up Project

As we did earlier, initialize a new project:

bash

```
mkdir todo-api
cd todo-api
npm init -y  # Initialize the project
```

Install the necessary dependencies:

bash

```
npm install express
```

Step 2: Create server.js

Create a server.js file and set up a basic Express server to handle CRUD operations for a to-do list.

javascript

```
const express = require('express');
const app = express();
const port = 3000;

app.use(express.json()); // Middleware to parse JSON
```

```
let todos = [
  { id: 1, task: 'Learn Node.js' },
  { id: 2, task: 'Build REST API' }
];

// Get all to-do items
app.get('/todos', (req, res) => {
  res.json(todos);
});

// Get a to-do item by ID
app.get('/todos/:id', (req, res) => {
  const todo = todos.find(t => t.id === parseInt(req.params.id));
  if (!todo) return res.status(404).send('To-Do not found');
  res.json(todo);
});

// Create a new to-do item
app.post('/todos', (req, res) => {
  const todo = { id: todos.length + 1, task: req.body.task };
  todos.push(todo);
  res.status(201).json(todo);
});

// Update a to-do item
app.put('/todos/:id', (req, res) => {
  const todo = todos.find(t => t.id === parseInt(req.params.id));
  if (!todo) return res.status(404).send('To-Do not found');
  todo.task = req.body.task;
  res.json(todo);
```

```
});

// Delete a to-do item
app.delete('/todos/:id', (req, res) => {
  const todoIndex = todos.findIndex(t => t.id === parseInt(req.params.id));
  if (todoIndex === -1) return res.status(404).send('To-Do not found');
  todos.splice(todoIndex, 1);
  res.status(204).send();
});

app.listen(port, () => {
  console.log(`To-Do API server running at http://localhost:${port}`);
});
```

Step 3: Running the Server

To run the server, simply execute:

bash

node server.js

You can now use tools like **Postman** or **cURL** to test the API:

- **GET /todos**: Retrieve all to-do items.
- **GET /todos/:id**: Retrieve a specific to-do item by ID.
- **POST /todos**: Create a new to-do item.
- **PUT /todos/:id**: Update an existing to-do item.
- **DELETE /todos/:id**: Delete a to-do item.

Summary

In this chapter, we introduced **Node.js** and **Express.js** and explored how they can be used to build back-end applications. We covered key concepts such as **RESTful APIs**, **CRUD operations**, and the importance of using a back-end framework for building efficient and scalable applications. We also built a **simple to-do API** using **Node.js** and **Express**, which allowed us to perform basic CRUD operations on a to-do list.

Node.js and Express.js are powerful tools for building fast, scalable, and real-time web applications, and this chapter provided a foundational understanding of how to create a basic back-end server to handle requests and interact with data.

Chapter 15: Introduction to Back-End Frameworks: Django

Django is a high-level **Python web framework** that encourages rapid development and clean, pragmatic design. It was created to help developers build web applications quickly, while keeping the codebase maintainable and scalable. In this chapter, we will explore **what Django is**, its built-in features, how to set up a Django project, and finally, we will walk through a **real-world example** of building a **simple blog** with Django.

What is Django and Why Use It?

Django is an open-source web framework written in **Python**. It follows the **Model-View-Template (MVT)** architectural pattern, similar to the Model-View-Controller (MVC) pattern commonly used in other frameworks. Django is designed to help developers build robust, secure, and scalable web applications in a fraction of the time it would take using traditional methods.

Why Use Django?

1. **Rapid Development**: Django comes with built-in features like an **admin interface**, **authentication system**, and **database ORM**, which significantly reduce the time and effort required to build web applications from scratch. With

Django, you can focus more on writing business logic than handling repetitive tasks.

2. **Built-in Admin Interface**: Django automatically generates an **admin interface** that allows you to manage the database, including adding, modifying, and deleting records, without needing to write custom code.

3. **Security**: Django has several built-in security features that help developers avoid common security vulnerabilities such as SQL injection, cross-site scripting (XSS), and cross-site request forgery (CSRF). It includes built-in mechanisms for user authentication, password management, and data validation.

4. **Scalability**: Django follows best practices for scalability and allows you to build complex applications that can handle large traffic volumes. It is widely used by large-scale websites such as **Instagram**, **Pinterest**, and **The Washington Post**.

5. **Comprehensive Documentation**: Django's official documentation is well-structured, easy to understand, and comprehensive. It provides thorough explanations for both beginners and experienced developers.

Django's Built-in Features: Authentication, Admin Interface, ORM

1. **Authentication**: Django provides a **built-in authentication system** that includes user login, logout, registration, and password management features. The system handles:

   o   User authentication and authorization.

   o   Password hashing and security.

   o   Session management.

This system is highly customizable and can be extended to include additional features such as email verification, social login, etc.

Example of a basic user authentication flow:

python

```python
from django.contrib.auth import authenticate, login
from django.shortcuts import render, redirect

def user_login(request):
    if request.method == 'POST':
        username = request.POST['username']
        password = request.POST['password']
        user = authenticate(request, username=username, password=password)
        if user is not None:
            login(request, user)
            return redirect('home')
        else:
            return render(request, 'login.html', {'error': 'Invalid credentials'})
```

```
return render(request, 'login.html')
```

2. **Admin Interface**: One of Django's standout features is its **automatically generated admin interface**. It allows you to quickly manage your models and database entries without writing additional code.

   To enable the admin interface, you simply register models in your admin.py file:

   python

   ```
   from django.contrib import admin
   from .models import Post
   ```

   ```
   admin.site.register(Post)
   ```

   This will create a user-friendly interface for managing Post entries, with the ability to add, edit, and delete posts.

3. **ORM (Object-Relational Mapping)**: Django comes with a powerful **ORM** that allows developers to interact with the database using Python objects instead of writing raw SQL queries. This makes database interactions easier and more Pythonic.

   Example of defining a simple Post model:

   python

```python
from django.db import models

class Post(models.Model):
    title = models.CharField(max_length=200)
    content = models.TextField()
    created_at = models.DateTimeField(auto_now_add=True)

    def __str__(self):
        return self.title
```

The ORM will automatically generate the necessary SQL to create and modify the database schema based on your model definitions. You can also perform CRUD operations on your models directly through Python code:

python

```python
post = Post.objects.create(title='My First Post', content='This is the content of the post.')
```

Setting Up a Django Project and Creating Views

To get started with Django, you'll first need to set up a new Django project and configure the necessary files.

1. **Setting Up a New Django Project**: To create a new Django project, first install Django using pip:

bash

```
pip install django
```

Next, create a new Django project:

```
bash
```

```
django-admin startproject myproject
cd myproject
```

Create a new Django app inside the project:

```
bash
```

```
python manage.py startapp blog
```

Add the blog app to the INSTALLED_APPS section in the settings.py file:

```
python
```

```
INSTALLED_APPS = [
    'django.contrib.admin',
    'django.contrib.auth',
    'django.contrib.contenttypes',
    'django.contrib.sessions',
    'django.contrib.messages',
    'django.contrib.staticfiles',
    'blog',
]
```

2. **Creating Views**: Django views are functions that receive a web request and return a web response. Views can be used

to render HTML templates, redirect users, or return other types of responses (such as JSON data for APIs).

Example of a simple view in views.py:

python

```
from django.shortcuts import render
from .models import Post

def home(request):
    posts = Post.objects.all()
    return render(request, 'home.html', {'posts': posts})
```

This view fetches all the Post objects from the database and renders the home.html template, passing the posts as context.

3. **Creating URLs**: You need to map views to specific URLs using the urls.py file. In your app's urls.py, add:

python

```
from django.urls import path
from . import views

urlpatterns = [
    path('', views.home, name='home'),
]
```

In the project-level urls.py file, include the app's URLs:

python

```python
from django.contrib import admin
from django.urls import path, include

urlpatterns = [
    path('admin/', admin.site.urls),
    path('', include('blog.urls')),
]
```

Real-World Example: Building a Simple Blog with Django

Now, let's build a **simple blog** using Django. We will define a Post model, create views to display and create blog posts, and use Django's built-in admin interface to manage posts.

Step 1: Define the Post Model

In models.py:

python

```python
from django.db import models

class Post(models.Model):
    title = models.CharField(max_length=200)
    content = models.TextField()
    created_at = models.DateTimeField(auto_now_add=True)

    def __str__(self):
        return self.title
```

Step 2: Create the Views

In views.py, create a view to display all posts and a form to add new posts:

python

```python
from django.shortcuts import render, redirect
from .models import Post
from .forms import PostForm

def home(request):
    posts = Post.objects.all()
    return render(request, 'home.html', {'posts': posts})

def add_post(request):
    if request.method == 'POST':
        form = PostForm(request.POST)
        if form.is_valid():
            form.save()
            return redirect('home')
    else:
        form = PostForm()
    return render(request, 'add_post.html', {'form': form})
```

Step 3: Create the Forms

In forms.py, define a form for creating posts:

python

```python
from django import forms
```

```
from .models import Post

class PostForm(forms.ModelForm):
    class Meta:
        model = Post
        fields = ['title', 'content']
```

Step 4: Create Templates

Create a home.html template to display the list of posts:

html

```
<h1>Blog Posts</h1>
<ul>
    {% for post in posts %}
      <li>
        <a href="#">{{ post.title }}</a>
        <p>{{ post.created_at }}</p>
      </li>
    {% endfor %}
</ul>


<a href="{% url 'add_post' %}">Add a new post</a>
```

Create an add_post.html template for the form:

html

```
<h1>Add New Post</h1>
<form method="post">
    {% csrf_token %}
    {{ form.as_p }}
```

```html
    <button type="submit">Save</button>
</form>
```

Step 5: Set Up URLs

In urls.py, map the views to URLs:

python

```python
from django.urls import path
from . import views

urlpatterns = [
    path('', views.home, name='home'),
    path('add/', views.add_post, name='add_post'),
]
```

Step 6: Admin Interface

To enable the admin interface for managing posts, register the Post model in admin.py:

python

```python
from django.contrib import admin
from .models import Post

admin.site.register(Post)
```

Step 7: Running the Server

Run the server:

bash

python manage.py runserver

You can now go to http://localhost:8000/ to view the blog and add new posts through the admin interface at http://localhost:8000/admin/.

Summary

In this chapter, we introduced **Django**, a powerful Python-based web framework, and explored its built-in features such as **authentication**, the **admin interface**, and the **ORM**. We walked through setting up a Django project, creating views, and defining models, and built a **simple blog** as a real-world example using these features.

Django's automatic admin interface, powerful ORM, and built-in security make it an excellent choice for building robust and scalable web applications. With this foundational knowledge, you can start developing full-fledged applications and take advantage of Django's built-in tools and libraries.

Chapter 16: Going Further with Django

In this chapter, we will delve deeper into **Django's Model-View-Template (MVT)** architecture, explore how to build **dynamic forms** and handle user requests, and cover the steps to **deploy Django applications**. We will also walk through a **real-world example** of building a **contact form** with Django, showcasing how to integrate forms into your application effectively.

Django's MVT Architecture (Model-View-Template)

Django follows the **Model-View-Template (MVT)** architecture, which is similar to the **Model-View-Controller (MVC)** pattern used by many other frameworks. However, Django's naming conventions differ slightly. Here's an overview of the three core components:

1. **Model**:
    o   The **Model** defines the data structure of the application, usually corresponding to a database table. It encapsulates the fields and behavior of the data and is responsible for querying and manipulating the database.

- o Django uses its **Object-Relational Mapping (ORM)** system to define models as Python classes, which are then mapped to database tables automatically.

Example:

python

```
from django.db import models

class Contact(models.Model):
    name = models.CharField(max_length=100)
    email = models.EmailField()
    message = models.TextField()
```

2. **View**:

- o The **View** is responsible for processing user requests and returning a response. It handles the business logic of the application, including interacting with models and preparing data for the template. In Django, a view is typically a function or a class-based view (CBV) that takes a request and returns a response.

Example:

python

```
from django.shortcuts import render
```

```python
from .models import Contact

def contact_view(request):
    if request.method == 'POST':
        name = request.POST['name']
        email = request.POST['email']
        message = request.POST['message']
        # Save data to the database
        Contact.objects.create(name=name,                    email=email,
message=message)
        return render(request, 'thank_you.html', {'name': name})
    return render(request, 'contact_form.html')
```

3. **Template**:

   o The **Template** is responsible for rendering HTML content to be displayed to the user. Templates are often written in Django's template language (DTL), which allows you to embed dynamic data, loops, and conditional logic into your HTML.

   Example:

   html

```html
<form method="POST">
    {% csrf_token %}
    <input type="text" name="name" placeholder="Your Name">
    <input type="email" name="email" placeholder="Your Email">
    <textarea            name="message"            placeholder="Your
Message"></textarea>
```

```
<button type="submit">Submit</button>
</form>
```

By using this architecture, Django enforces a clear separation of concerns between the data (Model), the logic (View), and the presentation (Template), making it easier to maintain and scale applications.

Building Dynamic Forms and Handling Requests

Django makes it easy to create **dynamic forms** for user input, manage form submissions, and process form data.

1. **Creating Forms**: Django provides the forms module to create form classes that handle validation, rendering, and submitting form data.

   Example of creating a simple form using Django's forms module:

   python

   ```python
   from django import forms

   class ContactForm(forms.Form):
       name = forms.CharField(max_length=100)
       email = forms.EmailField()
       message = forms.CharField(widget=forms.Textarea)
   ```

   In the view, you can handle form submissions and validation:

python

```python
from django.shortcuts import render
from .forms import ContactForm

def contact_view(request):
    if request.method == 'POST':
        form = ContactForm(request.POST)
        if form.is_valid():
            # Process the form data (e.g., save to database)
            name = form.cleaned_data['name']
            email = form.cleaned_data['email']
            message = form.cleaned_data['message']
            return render(request, 'thank_you.html', {'name': name})
    else:
        form = ContactForm()

    return render(request, 'contact_form.html', {'form': form})
```

2. **Form Validation**: Django's form classes automatically handle validation for fields like **required fields**, **minimum/maximum lengths**, and **format validation** (e.g., email format). You can also add custom validation by overriding the clean() method in the form class.

Example of adding custom validation:

python

```python
def clean_message(self):
```

```
message = self.cleaned_data.get('message')
if len(message) < 10:
    raise forms.ValidationError('Message must be at least 10 characters
long.')
return message
```

3. **Rendering Forms**: In your template, you can render the form fields and handle form errors:

html

```html
<form method="POST">
    {% csrf_token %}
    {{ form.as_p }}
    <button type="submit">Submit</button>
</form>

{% if form.errors %}
<ul>
    {% for field in form %}
        {% for error in field.errors %}
            <li>{{ error }}</li>
        {% endfor %}
    {% endfor %}
</ul>
{% endif %}
```

Deploying Django Applications

After building a Django application, the next step is deploying it to a production server so that users can access it over the internet. Here are the common steps for deploying a Django application:

1. **Prepare the Application for Production**:
   - Set DEBUG = False in settings.py.
   - Set **allowed hosts** in ALLOWED_HOSTS (e.g., ALLOWED_HOSTS = ['yourdomain.com', 'localhost']).
   - Ensure that static files are being served properly (Django needs to collect static files into a central location for production).

2. **Database Configuration**:
   - Use a production database (like PostgreSQL or MySQL) instead of SQLite.
   - Update DATABASES settings in settings.py to point to your production database.

3. **Web Server Setup**:
   - Deploy Django with a **web server** like **Gunicorn** or **uWSGI**.
   - Use **Nginx** or **Apache** as a reverse proxy to handle incoming traffic and pass it to the Django application.

4. **Static and Media Files**:
   - Run the following command to collect all static files in one directory:

   bash

python manage.py collectstatic

5. **Deploy to Cloud**:
   - Platforms like **Heroku, AWS Elastic Beanstalk,** and **DigitalOcean** offer simple ways to deploy Django applications.
   - Ensure you have a .env file for sensitive data such as API keys and database credentials.

Real-World Example: Building a Contact Form with Django

Let's now walk through a real-world example of building a **contact form** in Django. Users will be able to submit their name, email, and message through a form, and the data will be processed and stored in the database.

Step 1: Define the Model: First, we'll define the Contact model to store the form data in the database.

python

```
# models.py
from django.db import models

class Contact(models.Model):
    name = models.CharField(max_length=100)
    email = models.EmailField()
```

```python
message = models.TextField()
submitted_at = models.DateTimeField(auto_now_add=True)

def __str__(self):
    return f'Contact from {self.name}'
```

Step 2: Create the Form: Next, we'll create a form to handle user input.

python

```python
# forms.py
from django import forms
from .models import Contact

class ContactForm(forms.ModelForm):
    class Meta:
        model = Contact
        fields = ['name', 'email', 'message']
```

Step 3: Create the View: We'll now define a view to handle form submissions.

python

```python
# views.py
from django.shortcuts import render, redirect
from .forms import ContactForm
from .models import Contact

def contact_view(request):
    if request.method == 'POST':
```

```python
    form = ContactForm(request.POST)
    if form.is_valid():
        form.save()  # Save the data to the database
        return redirect('thank_you')  # Redirect to a "Thank You" page
    else:
        form = ContactForm()

    return render(request, 'contact_form.html', {'form': form})
```

Step 4: Create the Template: Now we'll create the template to render the form and display any validation errors.

html

```html
<!-- contact_form.html -->
<h1>Contact Us</h1>
<form method="POST">
    {% csrf_token %}
    {{ form.as_p }}
    <button type="submit">Submit</button>
</form>

{% if form.errors %}
<ul>
    {% for field in form %}
        {% for error in field.errors %}
            <li>{{ error }}</li>
        {% endfor %}
    {% endfor %}
</ul>
{% endif %}
```

Step 5: Set Up URLs: In urls.py, we define the route to handle the contact form:

python

```
# urls.py
from django.urls import path
from . import views

urlpatterns = [
    path('contact/', views.contact_view, name='contact_form'),
]
```

Step 6: Running the Server: To see the form in action, run the server:

bash

```
python manage.py runserver
```

You can now visit http://localhost:8000/contact/ to view the contact form. When users submit the form, the data will be saved in the database.

Summary

In this chapter, we went further with Django by exploring its **Model-View-Template (MVT)** architecture, which separates the application logic into models, views, and templates, ensuring maintainability and scalability. We learned how to create **dynamic forms**, validate user input, and handle form submissions in Django.

We also discussed the process of **deploying Django applications**, covering important steps like preparing the app for production, setting up databases, and using web servers like Gunicorn and Nginx. Finally, we built a **real-world contact form** that allows users to submit their details and store them in a database.

By mastering these concepts, you can create robust, secure, and scalable web applications with Django that handle dynamic data and user interactions.

Chapter 17: Introduction to Back-End Frameworks: Ruby on Rails

Ruby on Rails, often referred to as **Rails**, is a powerful web application framework built using the Ruby programming language. It provides an opinionated, convention-over-configuration approach to building web applications, enabling developers to create robust, scalable, and maintainable applications quickly. In this chapter, we will explore **what Ruby on Rails is**, the **MVC architecture** that drives its structure, the **built-in tools** like **ActiveRecord** and **scaffolding**, and finally, we'll walk through a **real-world example** of building a **user registration system** using Ruby on Rails.

What is Ruby on Rails and Why Use It?

Ruby on Rails is an open-source web application framework that prioritizes **convention over configuration**, allowing developers to spend less time setting up the infrastructure and more time writing application logic. It is designed to follow the **Model-View-Controller (MVC)** architecture, which separates the concerns of an application into three distinct layers.

Why Use Ruby on Rails?

1. **Rapid Development**:

- o Rails allows developers to build web applications quickly by providing pre-built templates, routing systems, and models. This reduces the amount of boilerplate code you need to write.
- o The **convention-over-configuration** principle in Rails means that there are sensible defaults for most configurations, so you don't have to make many decisions about how to set up your app.

2. **Built-in Tools**:

- o Rails comes with a rich set of built-in tools, including **ActiveRecord** for working with databases, **scaffolding** to quickly generate application components, and **ActionView** for rendering views.
- o These tools allow you to focus on business logic instead of dealing with mundane tasks like setting up routing, validation, and database operations.

3. **Active Community and Ecosystem**:

- o Rails has a strong, active community that contributes to a vast ecosystem of gems (libraries) and plugins. There are gems for nearly everything, from authentication to payments and testing.

4. **Scalability**:

- o Although Rails is often perceived as best for small to medium-sized applications, it is also used by large-scale applications such as **GitHub** and **Airbnb**, demonstrating its scalability and ability to handle large amounts of traffic.

5. **Security**:

   o Rails includes several security features out of the box, such as protection against SQL injection, cross-site scripting (XSS), and cross-site request forgery (CSRF). It also has built-in support for encryption and user authentication.

Understanding Rails Conventions: MVC Architecture

Ruby on Rails follows the **Model-View-Controller (MVC)** architecture, which divides the application into three main components:

1. **Model**:

   o The **Model** is responsible for the application's data and business logic. In Rails, models are typically connected to database tables, and they handle validation, associations, and querying the database.

   o Models in Rails use **ActiveRecord**, which is an **Object-Relational Mapping (ORM)** system. ActiveRecord abstracts the database interactions and allows you to query and manipulate data using Ruby objects.

Example of a simple User model:

ruby

```
class User < ApplicationRecord
  validates :name, presence: true
  validates :email, presence: true, uniqueness: true
end
```

2. **View**:

   o The **View** is responsible for rendering the user interface of the application. In Rails, views are typically written in **HTML**, with embedded **Ruby** code for dynamic content. Rails uses the **ERB (Embedded Ruby)** templating engine for generating dynamic HTML.

   Example of a simple view template (app/views/users/show.html.erb):

   erb

   ```
   <h1><%= @user.name %></h1>
   <p>Email: <%= @user.email %></p>
   ```

3. **Controller**:

   o The **Controller** handles user requests, interacts with the model to retrieve data, and sends the appropriate view back to the user. In Rails, controllers are responsible for managing the flow of data between the model and the view.

Example of a UsersController:

ruby

```
class UsersController < ApplicationController
 def show
  @user = User.find(params[:id])
 end
end
```

By following the **MVC architecture**, Rails helps maintain clean code separation and organizes application logic in a way that is easy to maintain and scale.

Working with Rails' Built-In Tools: ActiveRecord, Scaffolding

1. **ActiveRecord**:
   o **ActiveRecord** is Rails' default ORM, and it enables you to work with databases in an object-oriented way. It automatically maps database tables to Ruby classes and allows you to perform CRUD operations using simple Ruby syntax.

   Basic ActiveRecord operations:

- o **Create**: User.create(name: 'Alice', email: 'alice@example.com')
- o **Read**: User.find(1) or User.where(name: 'Alice')
- o **Update**: user.update(email: 'newemail@example.com')
- o **Delete**: user.destroy

Example of creating a new record:

ruby

```
user = User.new(name: 'John Doe', email: 'john.doe@example.com')
user.save
```

2. **Scaffolding**:

- o **Scaffolding** is a Rails feature that generates all the necessary files (models, views, controllers, migrations) for a specific resource with a single command. It is a great tool for rapid application development and getting started quickly.

Example of generating a scaffold for a User resource:

bash

```
rails generate scaffold User name:string email:string
```

This command generates:

- o A **model** (user.rb).
- o A **controller** (users_controller.rb).

- o Views for **CRUD operations** (e.g., index.html.erb, new.html.erb).
- o A **migration** file to create the users table in the database.

After running the command, you need to migrate the database:

bash

rails db:migrate

The scaffold will provide a fully functional CRUD interface for the User resource, which you can customize as needed.

Real-World Example: Building a User Registration System with Ruby on Rails

Let's now walk through a **real-world example** of building a **user registration system** in Ruby on Rails. This system will allow users to register by providing their name and email, and the data will be stored in a database.

Step 1: Create a New Rails Project

Start by creating a new Rails project:

bash

```
rails new user_registration_system
cd user_registration_system
```

Step 2: Generate the User Scaffold

Next, generate a scaffold for the User resource:

bash

```
rails generate scaffold User name:string email:string
```

This will generate all the necessary files for the User resource, including the model, controller, views, and database migration.

Step 3: Migrate the Database

Run the migration to create the users table in the database:

bash

```
rails db:migrate
```

Step 4: Set Up Routes

Open config/routes.rb and define the routes for the user registration system:

ruby

```
Rails.application.routes.draw do
  resources :users
  root 'users#index'
end
```

Step 5: Customize the Views

You can customize the generated views to match your requirements. For example, modify app/views/users/_form.html.erb to make the form look better:

erb

```
<%= form_with(model: user, local: true) do |form| %>
  <% if user.errors.any? %>
    <div id="error_explanation">
      <h2><%= pluralize(user.errors.count, "error") %> prohibited this user from being saved:</h2>
      <ul>
        <% user.errors.full_messages.each do |message| %>
        <li><%= message %></li>
        <% end %>
      </ul>
    </div>
  <% end %>

  <div class="field">
    <%= form.label :name %>
    <%= form.text_field :name %>
  </div>

  <div class="field">
    <%= form.label :email %>
    <%= form.text_field :email %>
  </div>

  <div class="actions">
```

```
<%= form.submit %>
  </div>
<% end %>
```

Step 6: Run the Rails Server

Now, you can run the server and visit the application in your browser:

bash

rails server

Go to http://localhost:3000/users to see the list of users and http://localhost:3000/users/new to register a new user.

Summary

In this chapter, we introduced **Ruby on Rails**, a powerful web application framework that follows the **Model-View-Controller (MVC)** architecture. We discussed Rails' built-in tools, including **ActiveRecord** for database management and **scaffolding** for rapid application development. We also built a **real-world example** of a **user registration system** that demonstrates how to handle user input, store data in a database, and display the results using Rails' default MVC pattern.

Ruby on Rails is a great choice for developers looking to build web applications quickly and efficiently, with its rich set of tools, conventions, and strong community support. With the knowledge gained in this chapter, you can now create a variety of applications using Rails and its powerful features.

Chapter 18: Introduction to Back-End Frameworks: Flask

Flask is a **micro web framework** written in **Python** that allows developers to build web applications quickly and with minimal setup. Unlike full-stack frameworks like Django, Flask provides just the essentials, leaving developers with the flexibility to choose their own tools for things like authentication, database management, and form handling. In this chapter, we will explore **what Flask is**, its **minimalistic approach** to web development, how to set up **routes**, **templates**, and **static files**, and build a **real-world example** of a **basic Flask blog application**.

What is Flask and Why Use It?

Flask is a lightweight and flexible web framework for building web applications. It was created by **Armin Ronacher** and is often described as a "micro" framework because it provides the basic tools for web development without enforcing specific project structures or requiring certain tools. Flask allows you to start small and scale up as needed, providing the building blocks to create custom web applications while giving you the freedom to pick and choose additional components.

Why Use Flask?

1. **Simplicity and Flexibility**:
   - Flask offers a simple API and follows a **minimalistic** approach. Unlike some larger frameworks, it doesn't come with a lot of built-in features that may not be required for every application. This allows developers to focus on the logic of their application and choose only the features they need.

2. **Extensibility**:
   - Flask is highly **extensible** and can integrate easily with various libraries and tools. Whether it's for handling database management (e.g., SQLAlchemy), authentication (e.g., Flask-Login), or form validation (e.g., Flask-WTF), Flask's modular approach lets you add functionality when needed.

3. **Minimal Setup**:
   - Flask is designed to get applications running with a minimal amount of configuration. It doesn't require complex configurations or the use of any ORM by default, allowing developers to get a basic app up and running with just a few lines of code.

4. **Large Community and Documentation**:
   - Flask has a large and active community, and the official documentation is thorough and beginner-friendly. Additionally, Flask is supported by a wide array of extensions and third-party tools.

5. **Perfect for Small to Medium Applications**:
   - o Flask is ideal for building small to medium-sized applications, APIs, or microservices. It's widely used for projects like RESTful APIs, prototypes, and apps with simple functionality.

Flask's Minimalistic Approach to Web Development

Flask follows a minimalistic approach to web development by providing the core essentials and leaving the rest up to the developer. Unlike frameworks like Django, which come with a lot of built-in features, Flask allows you to choose which components you want to use for your app.

1. **Routing**:
   - o Flask provides a simple routing mechanism where you can map URLs to Python functions. You can easily create routes for different HTTP methods like GET and POST.

   Example of a route:

   python

```python
@app.route('/')
def home():
    return "Hello, Flask!"
```

2. **Request and Response Handling**:
   - Flask allows you to easily access incoming HTTP requests and manipulate outgoing responses. You can extract form data, query parameters, JSON, and more from incoming requests.

3. **Template Rendering**:
   - Flask integrates with the **Jinja2** templating engine, allowing you to render dynamic HTML pages. It provides easy-to-use features like template inheritance, conditionals, and loops, making it easier to create views with dynamic content.

4. **Static Files**:
   - Flask can serve static files like images, CSS, and JavaScript. By default, static files are placed in the static/ directory and are accessible via a URL path (/static/).

5. **Modularity**:
   - Flask allows you to structure your app in a modular way, making it easier to break it down into reusable components (e.g., blueprints, extensions).

Setting Up Routes, Templates, and Static Files in Flask

1. **Setting Up Routes**:

- o In Flask, routes are defined using the @app.route decorator. Routes map URLs to Python functions (views) that will be executed when the user accesses that URL.

Example of setting up multiple routes:

python

```
from flask import Flask, render_template

app = Flask(__name__)

@app.route('/')
def home():
    return render_template('home.html')

@app.route('/about')
def about():
    return render_template('about.html')

if __name__ == '__main__':
    app.run(debug=True)
```

In the example above, we have two routes: / and /about. Each route returns an HTML page rendered from a template.

2. **Setting Up Templates**:
   - o Flask uses the **Jinja2** templating engine to render dynamic HTML. Templates are stored in the

templates/ directory, and you can use Jinja2 syntax to insert variables, loops, and conditionals.

Example of a simple template (home.html):

html

```
<!DOCTYPE html>
<html lang="en">
<head>
  <meta charset="UTF-8">
  <title>Home Page</title>
</head>
<body>
  <h1>Welcome to the Flask Blog</h1>
  <p>This is the home page.</p>
</body>
</html>
```

In the home() view function, we use render_template('home.html') to render this HTML page.

3. **Setting Up Static Files**:
   - Flask automatically serves static files from the static/ directory. For example, if you have a styles.css file in static/css/, you can reference it in your templates as follows:

Example of including a CSS file in home.html:

html

```
<link rel="stylesheet" href="{{ url_for('static', filename='css/styles.css')
}}">
```

Real-World Example: Creating a Basic Flask Blog Application

Let's now create a simple **Flask blog** application that allows users to view blog posts and submit new posts.

Step 1: Setting Up the Flask Project

Create a new directory for your project and navigate into it:

bash

```
mkdir flask_blog
cd flask_blog
```

Set up a virtual environment and install Flask:

bash

```
python3 -m venv venv
source venv/bin/activate  # On Windows, use venv\Scripts\activate
pip install flask
```

Create a file called app.py to define your Flask app.

Step 2: Define the Flask App

In app.py, set up the basic routes for viewing and creating blog posts:

python

```python
from flask import Flask, render_template, request, redirect

app = Flask(__name__)

# In-memory blog posts
posts = [
    {'title': 'My First Post', 'content': 'This is the content of my first post.'},
    {'title': 'Flask is Awesome', 'content': 'Flask makes it easy to build web apps.'},
]

@app.route('/')
def home():
    return render_template('home.html', posts=posts)

@app.route('/add', methods=['GET', 'POST'])
def add_post():
    if request.method == 'POST':
        title = request.form['title']
        content = request.form['content']
        posts.append({'title': title, 'content': content})
        return redirect('/')
    return render_template('add_post.html')

if __name__ == '__main__':
    app.run(debug=True)
```

Step 3: Set Up Templates

1. **Home Page Template (home.html):**

html

```html
<!DOCTYPE html>
<html lang="en">
<head>
    <meta charset="UTF-8">
    <title>Flask Blog</title>
</head>
<body>
    <h1>Welcome to the Flask Blog</h1>
    <a href="/add">Add a new post</a>
    <ul>
        {% for post in posts %}
          <li>
             <h2>{{ post.title }}</h2>
             <p>{{ post.content }}</p>
          </li>
        {% endfor %}
    </ul>
</body>
</html>
```

2. **Add Post Template (add_post.html):**

html

```html
<!DOCTYPE html>
<html lang="en">
<head>
    <meta charset="UTF-8">
```

217

```
        <title>Add a New Post</title>
    </head>
    <body>
        <h1>Add a New Post</h1>
        <form method="POST">
            <label for="title">Title</label>
            <input type="text" name="title" required><br><br>
            <label for="content">Content</label><br>
            <textarea name="content" required></textarea><br><br>
            <button type="submit">Submit</button>
        </form>
    </body>
</html>
```

Step 4: Running the Flask App

Now that we have our app set up, run the Flask development server:

bash

python app.py

Visit http://localhost:5000/ in your browser to view the homepage, and go to http://localhost:5000/add to add new blog posts.

Summary

In this chapter, we introduced **Flask**, a lightweight Python web framework that emphasizes simplicity and flexibility. We explored its **minimalistic approach** to web development, covering essential concepts like **routes, templates,** and **static files**.

We also built a **real-world Flask blog application**, demonstrating how to set up routes for viewing and creating blog posts, and using templates to render dynamic HTML. Flask's simplicity, extensibility, and modularity make it an excellent choice for building small to medium-sized web applications and APIs.

With Flask, you can quickly prototype web applications while having the freedom to add additional functionality as needed, making it a versatile tool for Python developers.

Chapter 19: API Development with Node.js and Express

In this chapter, we will explore the development of **RESTful APIs** using **Node.js** and **Express**. REST (Representational State Transfer) APIs are the backbone of modern web applications, enabling communication between the server and clients using standard HTTP methods. We'll walk through setting up **CRUD operations** (Create, Read, Update, and Delete) in Node.js with Express, how to test your API using **Postman**, and build a **real-world example** of a **user management system** through the API.

What is REST API and Why It Is Essential?

A **REST API** (Representational State Transfer API) is a set of rules and conventions for building web services that allow clients (such as browsers or mobile apps) to interact with the server. REST is based on HTTP methods and uses the URL to represent resources, while the HTTP methods define the actions that can be performed on those resources.

Key Characteristics of REST APIs:

1. **Stateless**: Each request from the client to the server must contain all the information necessary to understand and

process the request. The server does not store any state between requests.

2. **Client-Server Architecture**: The client (front-end) and server (back-end) communicate over HTTP. The server provides the resources, and the client consumes them.

3. **Uniform Interface**: REST APIs use a standardized set of operations that are understood by clients and servers, making it easier to develop and integrate web services.

4. **Resource-Based**: Each resource (e.g., user, post, comment) is identified by a URL. The resource can be represented in various formats, such as JSON or XML.

5. **Use of HTTP Methods**: The four primary HTTP methods used in RESTful APIs are:
   - **GET**: Retrieve data from the server.
   - **POST**: Create new data on the server.
   - **PUT/PATCH**: Update existing data on the server.
   - **DELETE**: Delete data on the server.

Why REST API Is Essential:

- **Decouples the Client and Server**: REST APIs allow clients and servers to evolve independently. The client doesn't need to know how the server processes data, and the server doesn't need to know the specifics of the client's interface.

- **Scalability**: REST APIs enable scalable systems. They allow multiple clients (web, mobile, IoT devices) to interact with the server in a consistent manner.

- **Standardization**: REST APIs follow standard HTTP protocols and methods, making it easier for developers to create and consume APIs. They are widely adopted in modern web development.

Setting Up CRUD Operations with Node.js and Express

Let's now create a simple REST API using **Node.js** and **Express** to handle **CRUD** operations for a user management system. The API will allow you to create, read, update, and delete user records.

Step 1: Set Up the Project

First, create a new directory and initialize a new Node.js project:

bash

```
mkdir user-api
cd user-api
npm init -y  # Initialize Node.js project
```

Install the necessary dependencies:

bash

```
npm install express body-parser
```

Step 2: Create the API Routes

Create a new file called app.js and set up the basic Express server:

javascript

```javascript
const express = require('express');
const bodyParser = require('body-parser');
const app = express();
const port = 3000;

// Middleware to parse JSON requests
app.use(bodyParser.json());

// Sample user data (in-memory storage for demonstration)
let users = [
  { id: 1, name: 'John Doe', email: 'john@example.com' },
  { id: 2, name: 'Jane Smith', email: 'jane@example.com' },
];

// GET /users: Retrieve all users
app.get('/users', (req, res) => {
  res.json(users);
});

// GET /users/:id: Retrieve a specific user by ID
app.get('/users/:id', (req, res) => {
  const user = users.find(u => u.id === parseInt(req.params.id));
  if (!user) {
    return res.status(404).send('User not found');
  }
}
```

```
  res.json(user);
});


// POST /users: Create a new user
app.post('/users', (req, res) => {
  const { name, email } = req.body;
  const user = {
    id: users.length + 1,
    name,
    email,
  };
  users.push(user);
  res.status(201).json(user);
});


// PUT /users/:id: Update an existing user
app.put('/users/:id', (req, res) => {
  const user = users.find(u => u.id === parseInt(req.params.id));
  if (!user) {
    return res.status(404).send('User not found');
  }
  user.name = req.body.name || user.name;
  user.email = req.body.email || user.email;
  res.json(user);
});


// DELETE /users/:id: Delete a user
app.delete('/users/:id', (req, res) => {
  const index = users.findIndex(u => u.id === parseInt(req.params.id));
  if (index === -1) {
```

```
  return res.status(404).send('User not found');
}
users.splice(index, 1);
res.status(204).send();
});


// Start the server
app.listen(port, () => {
  console.log(`Server running at http://localhost:${port}`);
});
```

Step 3: Test the API

To test your API, run the server:

bash

```
node app.js
```

You can now test the API using **Postman** or **cURL** by sending the following requests:

- **GET /users**: Retrieve all users.
- **GET /users/:id**: Retrieve a specific user by ID.
- **POST /users**: Create a new user (send a JSON body with name and email).
- **PUT /users/:id**: Update a specific user's information.
- **DELETE /users/:id**: Delete a user.

Example of testing with **Postman**:

1. **GET /users**: Open Postman and make a GET request to http://localhost:3000/users. This will return a list of all users.

2. **POST /users**: Make a POST request to http://localhost:3000/users with the body:

   json

   ```
   {
    "name": "Alice Johnson",
    "email": "alice@example.com"
   }
   ```

   This will create a new user and return the newly created user object.

3. **PUT /users/:id**: Make a PUT request to http://localhost:3000/users/1 with the body:

   json

   ```
   {
    "name": "John Doe Updated",
    "email": "john_updated@example.com"
   }
   ```

   This will update the user with ID 1.

4. **DELETE /users/:id**: Make a DELETE request to http://localhost:3000/users/2 to delete the user with ID 2.

API Testing with Postman

Postman is an excellent tool for testing APIs. It allows you to make HTTP requests, view responses, and check the status codes. To test the API, follow these steps:

1. **Install Postman**: Download and install Postman from Postman's official website.

2. **Test the GET Request**:
   - Open Postman and create a new GET request.
   - Enter the URL: http://localhost:3000/users to fetch the list of users.
   - Click on "Send", and you should see the response containing the list of users.

3. **Test the POST Request**:
   - Change the request type to POST.
   - Enter the URL: http://localhost:3000/users.
   - In the "Body" tab, select raw and choose JSON as the format. Enter the following data:

   json

   ```json
   {
   "name": "Alice",
   "email": "alice@example.com"
   }
   ```

- o Click "Send", and you should receive a response with the newly created user.

4. **Test the PUT Request**:
    - o Change the request type to PUT.
    - o Enter the URL: http://localhost:3000/users/1 (replace 1 with the appropriate user ID).
    - o In the "Body" tab, enter the updated data:

    json

    ```
    {
      "name": "Alice Updated",
      "email": "alice_updated@example.com"
    }
    ```

    - o Click "Send", and the user information should be updated.

5. **Test the DELETE Request**:
    - o Change the request type to DELETE.
    - o Enter the URL: http://localhost:3000/users/1.
    - o Click "Send", and the user should be deleted.

Real-World Example: Developing a User Management System with API

In this section, we have developed a **user management system** API using **Node.js** and **Express** that supports all **CRUD operations**. This system allows for:

- **Creating new users**.
- **Retrieving user information**.
- **Updating user details**.
- **Deleting users**.

Why use Node.js and Express for APIs?

- **Speed**: Node.js is designed for high-performance I/O operations, making it ideal for handling numerous API requests.
- **Ease of Use**: Express is a minimal framework that provides just the essentials, allowing you to focus on building the API.
- **Scalability**: Node.js is highly scalable, which means this API can handle a large number of requests as your application grows.

Summary

In this chapter, we covered the essentials of **RESTful API development** using **Node.js** and **Express**. We learned about **CRUD operations**, how to set up routes, handle user requests, and tested the API using **Postman**. We also developed a **real-world user management system API**, demonstrating how to build an API that can create, read, update, and delete user records.

By using **Node.js** and **Express**, you can quickly build powerful APIs for modern web applications. With Postman, testing and debugging these APIs becomes efficient and straightforward, enabling you to deliver high-quality, reliable services.

Chapter 20: Introduction to Full-Stack Development

Full-stack development refers to the development of both the **front-end** (client-side) and **back-end** (server-side) parts of a web application. A full-stack developer is capable of handling everything from the user interface to the server, databases, and APIs. In this chapter, we will explore **what full-stack development is**, the **different types of technology stacks** such as **MERN, MEAN**, and others, how **front-end and back-end frameworks** work together, and finally, we'll walk through a **real-world example** of building a full-stack web app using **React** for the front-end and **Node.js** for the back-end.

What is Full-Stack Development?

Full-stack development refers to the development of both the **front-end** and **back-end** components of a web application:

1. **Front-End (Client-Side)**:
    o The front-end is everything the user interacts with on a website or web app. It includes the layout, design, structure, and behavior of the page.

- o Technologies commonly used for front-end development include **HTML, CSS, JavaScript**, and frameworks like **React, Vue.js**, and **Angular**.

2. **Back-End (Server-Side)**:
   - o The back-end is responsible for the functionality behind the scenes—such as handling data, processing requests, interacting with databases, and managing authentication and authorization.
   - o Back-end development typically involves technologies like **Node.js, Python** (Django, Flask), **Ruby on Rails, Java**, and database management systems like **MongoDB, MySQL**, and **PostgreSQL**.

Full-stack developers are skilled in both areas, which allows them to create complete applications that handle both the user interface and the server-side functionality. These developers are also proficient in connecting the front-end with the back-end through APIs, managing databases, and ensuring that the system functions smoothly.

The Difference Between MERN, MEAN, and Other Stacks

In full-stack development, a **technology stack** is a collection of technologies used to build a web application. **MERN** and **MEAN** are popular tech stacks that focus on JavaScript-based technologies. Let's dive into the main differences between these stacks:

1. **MERN Stack**:
   - o **M**: MongoDB (database)
   - o **E**: Express.js (back-end web framework)
   - o **R**: React (front-end JavaScript library)
   - o **N**: Node.js (runtime environment)

Key Features:

   - o **MongoDB**: A NoSQL database that stores data in a flexible, JSON-like format. It works well with JavaScript-based technologies.
   - o **Express.js**: A minimal, unopinionated web framework for Node.js that simplifies building web servers and APIs.
   - o **React**: A JavaScript library for building user interfaces, particularly single-page applications (SPA).
   - o **Node.js**: A JavaScript runtime that allows you to run JavaScript on the server-side.

MERN is ideal for developers who prefer **React** for building dynamic, component-based user interfaces and want to use JavaScript for both the client and server-side code.

2. **MEAN Stack**:
    - **M**: MongoDB (database)
    - **E**: Express.js (back-end web framework)
    - **A**: Angular (front-end framework)
    - **N**: Node.js (runtime environment)

Key Features:

- **Angular**: A powerful front-end framework for building dynamic single-page applications (SPA). Unlike React, Angular is a full-fledged framework with tools for building entire applications.
- **MongoDB**, **Express.js**, and **Node.js** are the same as in the MERN stack.

MEAN is preferred by developers who like the structure and features provided by **Angular**, such as two-way data binding and dependency injection.

3. **Other Stacks**:
    - **LAMP Stack**: Linux (OS), Apache (web server), MySQL (database), PHP (server-side scripting). This stack is often used with traditional web applications.
    - **JAMstack**: JavaScript, APIs, and Markup. This stack focuses on decoupling the front-end from the back-end and using APIs to fetch data.

Different stacks are used based on the requirements of the project. Some stacks are more suitable for single-page applications, while others are better suited for traditional web apps.

How Front-End and Back-End Frameworks Work Together

In full-stack development, the **front-end** and **back-end** frameworks need to work together seamlessly to create a unified application. Here's how they interact:

1. **The Front-End**:
   - The front-end is responsible for the user interface and user experience (UI/UX). It makes requests to the back-end via HTTP methods (GET, POST, PUT, DELETE).
   - Modern front-end frameworks like **React** or **Angular** communicate with the back-end using **AJAX** (Asynchronous JavaScript and XML) or **fetch** API to send and receive data without reloading the page.
   - The data is typically exchanged in **JSON** format, making it easier for both the front-end and back-end to handle the data.
2. **The Back-End**:

o The back-end is responsible for handling business logic, interacting with databases, and providing APIs for the front-end to fetch data.

o **Node.js** with **Express** or any other back-end framework provides the routes, handles HTTP requests, interacts with databases, and sends the appropriate data back to the front-end.

Example of interaction:

o The front-end sends a request to the back-end to fetch a list of blog posts using fetch().

o The back-end (Node.js with Express) processes the request, queries the database (MongoDB, for example), and returns the data in a JSON format.

o The front-end receives the JSON data and updates the user interface accordingly.

Example Workflow:

- **Front-End (React)** sends a GET request to the back-end to fetch a list of blog posts.
- **Back-End (Node.js/Express)** processes the request, fetches data from MongoDB, and returns the data as a JSON response.

- **Front-End (React)** receives the JSON data and updates the UI by rendering the blog posts on the page.

Real-World Example: Building a Full-Stack Web App with React and Node.js

Let's walk through the creation of a **full-stack web app** that involves **React** for the front-end and **Node.js/Express** for the back-end. This will be a **simple blog application** where users can view, create, and delete blog posts.

Step 1: Setting Up the Project

We will set up two separate projects: one for the front-end and one for the back-end.

1. **Create the Back-End (Node.js/Express)**:
   - Initialize a new directory for the back-end:

   bash

   ```
   mkdir backend
   cd backend
   npm init -y  # Initialize Node.js project
   npm install express mongoose body-parser
   ```

   - Create a file server.js for the Express app:

```javascript

const express = require('express');
const mongoose = require('mongoose');
const bodyParser = require('body-parser');
const app = express();

// Middleware
app.use(bodyParser.json());

// MongoDB connection
mongoose.connect('mongodb://localhost:27017/fullstackdb', {
useNewUrlParser: true, useUnifiedTopology: true });

// Define a schema and model for blog posts
const Post = mongoose.model('Post', {
  title: String,
  content: String,
});

// API to get all posts
app.get('/posts', async (req, res) => {
  const posts = await Post.find();
  res.json(posts);
});

// API to create a new post
app.post('/posts', async (req, res) => {
  const post = new Post(req.body);
  await post.save();
```

```
  res.status(201).json(post);
});

// Start the server
app.listen(5000, () => {
  console.log('Server running on http://localhost:5000');
});
```

- o Start the back-end server:

bash

node server.js

2. **Create the Front-End (React)**:
- o Initialize a new React app:

bash

```
npx create-react-app frontend
cd frontend
```

- o Install Axios for making HTTP requests:

bash

npm install axios

- o Create a component for displaying and adding blog posts:

javascript

```javascript
// src/Blog.js
import React, { useState, useEffect } from 'react';
import axios from 'axios';

function Blog() {
  const [posts, setPosts] = useState([]);
  const [title, setTitle] = useState('');
  const [content, setContent] = useState('');

  // Fetch posts
  useEffect(() => {
    axios.get('http://localhost:5000/posts')
      .then(response => setPosts(response.data))
      .catch(error => console.error(error));
  }, []);

  // Add a new post
  const addPost = () => {
    const newPost = { title, content };
    axios.post('http://localhost:5000/posts', newPost)
      .then(response => setPosts([...posts, response.data]))
      .catch(error => console.error(error));
  };

  return (
    <div>
      <h1>Blog Posts</h1>
      <div>
```

```jsx
      {posts.map(post => (
        <div key={post._id}>
          <h3>{post.title}</h3>
          <p>{post.content}</p>
        </div>
      ))}
    </div>
    <h2>Add New Post</h2>
    <input
      type="text"
      value={title}
      onChange={e => setTitle(e.target.value)}
      placeholder="Post title"
    />
    <textarea
      value={content}
      onChange={e => setContent(e.target.value)}
      placeholder="Post content"
    />
    <button onClick={addPost}>Add Post</button>
    </div>
  );
}

export default Blog;
```

   o   **Run the React app:**

bash

npm start

Summary

In this chapter, we introduced **full-stack development** and discussed the different technology stacks, such as **MERN** and **MEAN**, which are widely used for building modern web applications. We also explored how **front-end and back-end frameworks** work together to create cohesive applications, focusing on **React** for the front-end and **Node.js/Express** for the back-end.

We then built a **full-stack blog application** that demonstrates how to set up **CRUD operations** with React and Node.js, allowing users to view and add blog posts. This example highlights the power and flexibility of full-stack development and the benefits of using JavaScript on both the client and server sides.

By mastering full-stack development, you will be able to create complete web applications that manage both user interfaces and back-end functionality.

Chapter 21: Authentication and Authorization in Web Applications

In modern web development, **authentication** and **authorization** are essential concepts for managing access to resources and ensuring that only the right users can perform specific actions. Understanding the difference between authentication and authorization, as well as the common methods used to implement them, is crucial for building secure web applications. In this chapter, we will provide an **overview of authentication vs authorization**, explore **common authentication methods** such as **Cookies, JWT (JSON Web Tokens)**, and **OAuth**, and implement a **real-world example** of **user login with JWT** in a **Node.js** application.

Overview of Authentication vs Authorization

1. **Authentication:**
   - **Authentication** is the process of verifying the identity of a user. This process ensures that the user is who they claim to be.
   - Typically, authentication is achieved by asking the user to provide a **username** and **password**, though there are other methods such as **biometrics, two-**

factor authentication (2FA), and **social login** (using Google, Facebook, etc.).

o   Authentication answers the question: **Who are you?**

Example: A user logs in by entering their email and password. The server checks the credentials and grants access if they match.

2. **Authorization**:

o   **Authorization** is the process of determining what actions or resources an authenticated user is allowed to access or perform. While authentication identifies the user, authorization ensures that they have the right permissions to access specific data or features.

o   Authorization typically involves assigning roles or permissions to users, such as **admin**, **user**, or **guest**, and restricting access to certain routes or data based on these roles.

o   Authorization answers the question: **What can you do?**

Example: Once the user is authenticated, authorization ensures that only users with the role of **admin** can access the admin dashboard or delete user data.

In summary:

- **Authentication** is about confirming who the user is.
- **Authorization** is about determining what the user is allowed to do.

Common Authentication Methods: Cookies, JWT, OAuth

1. **Cookies**:
   - o **Cookies** are small pieces of data stored by the browser on the client-side. When a user logs in, the server sends a cookie that contains a session identifier. This cookie is sent with each subsequent request to the server, allowing the server to recognize the user and maintain the session.
   - o **Advantages**: Cookies are simple to implement and widely supported by browsers.
   - o **Disadvantages**: Cookies are vulnerable to **cross-site scripting (XSS)** and **cross-site request forgery (CSRF)** attacks if not handled correctly.
2. **JWT (JSON Web Tokens)**:
   - o **JWT** is a compact, URL-safe token format used to securely transmit information between the client and server. A JWT consists of three parts: a **header**, a **payload**, and a **signature**. The payload can contain claims about the user (e.g., user ID, roles, expiration

time), and the signature is used to verify the token's authenticity.

- o **Advantages**: JWT is stateless, meaning that the server does not need to store any session data. It's also more flexible, as the client can send the token in headers, URLs, or cookies.
- o **Disadvantages**: JWT tokens can be vulnerable if the secret key is compromised, and they may need to be manually invalidated (e.g., by implementing token expiration).

JWT Flow:

4. The user logs in and sends a request with credentials (e.g., email and password).

5. If the credentials are valid, the server generates a JWT and sends it back to the client.

6. The client stores the JWT (usually in local storage or a cookie) and includes it in the Authorization header of future requests to authenticate API calls.

3. **OAuth**:
   - o **OAuth** is a protocol for authorization that allows users to grant third-party applications limited access to their resources without sharing their credentials.
   - o Commonly used for **social logins** (e.g., logging in with Google or Facebook), OAuth allows users to

authenticate using their existing credentials from trusted services.

- ○ **OAuth Flow**:
  1. The user is redirected to an external authentication provider (e.g., Google).
  2. The provider asks the user to grant permission to the third-party app.
  3. Once authorized, the provider sends an authorization code back to the app.
  4. The app exchanges the authorization code for an access token, which it can use to access the user's data.

Advantages: OAuth provides secure delegation of access and allows users to log in without creating new accounts or sharing passwords. **Disadvantages**: OAuth setup can be complex, and access tokens may need to be refreshed periodically.

Real-World Example: Implementing User Login with JWT in Node.js

Let's implement a **user login system with JWT** in **Node.js** and **Express**. This system will authenticate users, generate a JWT, and allow users to make authenticated requests using the token.

Step 1: Set Up the Node.js Project

Start by creating a new project directory and initializing it:

bash

```
mkdir jwt-auth
cd jwt-auth
npm init -y
```

Install the necessary dependencies:

bash

```
npm install express jsonwebtoken bcryptjs body-parser
```

Step 2: Create the User Model and Route for Registration

We will first create a basic **User model** to simulate user data. For simplicity, we will use **bcryptjs** to hash passwords.

Create a file called app.js:

javascript

```
const express = require('express');
const jwt = require('jsonwebtoken');
const bcrypt = require('bcryptjs');
const bodyParser = require('body-parser');
const app = express();
const PORT = 3000;


// Dummy user data (in-memory storage)
```

```
const users = [];

// Middleware
app.use(bodyParser.json());

// Secret key for JWT
const JWT_SECRET = 'your_jwt_secret';

// Registration route
app.post('/register', (req, res) => {
  const { username, password } = req.body;

  // Check if user already exists
  const userExists = users.find(user => user.username === username);
  if (userExists) return res.status(400).send('User already exists');

  // Hash password and save user
  const hashedPassword = bcrypt.hashSync(password, 10);
  const newUser = { username, password: hashedPassword };
  users.push(newUser);

  res.status(201).send('User registered');
});

// Login route
app.post('/login', (req, res) => {
  const { username, password } = req.body;

  // Find user
  const user = users.find(u => u.username === username);
```

```
if (!user) return res.status(400).send('User not found');

// Compare password
const isPasswordValid = bcrypt.compareSync(password, user.password);
if (!isPasswordValid) return res.status(400).send('Invalid password');

// Create JWT token
const token = jwt.sign({ username: user.username }, JWT_SECRET, {
expiresIn: '1h' });

  res.json({ token });
});

// Protected route
app.get('/dashboard', (req, res) => {
  const token = req.header('Authorization')?.replace('Bearer ', '');

  if (!token) return res.status(401).send('Access denied');

  try {
    const decoded = jwt.verify(token, JWT_SECRET);
    res.json({ message: `Welcome ${decoded.username}` });
  } catch (err) {
    res.status(400).send('Invalid token');
  }
});

// Start the server
app.listen(PORT, () => {
  console.log(`Server running on http://localhost:${PORT}`);
```

});

In this code:

- We have a simple **in-memory database** (users array) to store user data.
- The /**register** route allows users to register by providing a username and password.
- The /**login** route validates user credentials, generates a JWT, and returns the token.
- The /**dashboard** route is protected, requiring a valid JWT for access.

Step 3: Testing the API with Postman

1. **Register a User**:
   - o Make a **POST** request to http://localhost:3000/register with the following body:

   json

   ```
   {
   "username": "testuser",
   "password": "password123"
   }
   ```

2. **Login**:
   - o Make a **POST** request to http://localhost:3000/login with the same credentials.

- o   You will receive a **JWT** in the response.

3. **Access Protected Route**:

   - o   To access the **/dashboard** route, make a **GET** request to http://localhost:3000/dashboard and include the **JWT** in the Authorization header as a **Bearer token**:

makefile

Authorization: Bearer <your_jwt_token>

Summary

In this chapter, we explored **authentication** and **authorization** in web applications, focusing on the difference between the two concepts and common authentication methods like **cookies, JWT, and OAuth**. We then demonstrated how to implement a **JWT-based login system** in **Node.js** using **Express**.

JWT provides a stateless, secure way to authenticate users and authorize their access to protected resources. By implementing JWT authentication, we can ensure that users are properly authenticated, and we can control access to different parts of the application based on their identity and roles.

With this understanding of authentication and authorization, you can now implement secure login systems and control access to your web applications effectively.

Chapter 22: Database Integration in Web Applications

Databases are fundamental to web applications, allowing them to store and retrieve data efficiently. In this chapter, we will explore **relational vs NoSQL databases**, learn about popular databases like **MySQL, PostgreSQL**, and **MongoDB**, and discuss how to integrate these databases into your web applications. Finally, we'll walk through a **real-world example** of building a **CRUD app** with **MongoDB** and **Express.js**.

Introduction to Relational vs NoSQL Databases

1. **Relational Databases (RDBMS):**
   - Relational databases use **tables** to store data in rows and columns, with relationships between the tables defined using **foreign keys**.
   - Data in relational databases is structured and follows a schema (predefined columns and data types).
   - Common examples of relational databases include **MySQL, PostgreSQL, SQLite**, and **Oracle**.

   Advantages of Relational Databases:

- o Strong **data integrity** and **consistency** due to the use of ACID properties (Atomicity, Consistency, Isolation, Durability).
- o Support for complex queries, transactions, and joins to handle relationships between tables.
- o Well-suited for applications that require structured data with clear relationships (e.g., e-commerce systems, banking apps).

Disadvantages:

- o Rigid schema: changing the schema of a relational database can be cumbersome.
- o Less flexibility in handling large-scale, unstructured, or semi-structured data.

2. **NoSQL Databases**:
   - o **NoSQL** databases are designed to handle large volumes of unstructured or semi-structured data. They provide flexible schemas and often scale horizontally, making them ideal for distributed systems.
   - o There are several types of NoSQL databases, including:
     - **Document-based** (e.g., **MongoDB**)
     - **Key-Value** (e.g., **Redis**)
     - **Column-family** (e.g., **Cassandra**)

- **Graph databases** (e.g., **Neo4j**)

Advantages of NoSQL Databases:

o **Schema flexibility**: NoSQL databases allow you to store data without a predefined schema, making them ideal for applications with rapidly changing or unstructured data.

o **Scalability**: NoSQL databases often provide **horizontal scaling**, allowing applications to handle massive amounts of data across multiple servers.

o **Performance**: NoSQL databases are optimized for read/write operations on large datasets.

Disadvantages:

o Lack of ACID compliance in some NoSQL databases, which may lead to consistency issues in some cases.

o NoSQL databases often require custom data models, which can increase development time for complex applications.

Working with MySQL, PostgreSQL, MongoDB

1. **MySQL**:

- MySQL is one of the most popular open-source **relational databases**. It uses SQL (Structured Query Language) to interact with the data and is well-suited for applications that require structured data and complex queries.
- MySQL provides **transactions**, **data integrity**, and **complex querying** with **JOINs**, making it ideal for use cases where relationships between entities are important.

Example of a MySQL query:

sql

```
SELECT * FROM users WHERE username = 'johndoe';
```

2. **PostgreSQL**:

- PostgreSQL is another powerful open-source **relational database**. It supports more advanced features than MySQL, including **ACID compliance**, **advanced indexing**, and **full-text search**.
- It is known for its **robustness**, **standards compliance**, and **extensibility**, making it a great choice for complex applications and data models.

Example of a PostgreSQL query:

sql

```
SELECT * FROM users WHERE email = 'johndoe@example.com';
```

3. **MongoDB**:

   o **MongoDB** is a **document-based NoSQL database**. It stores data in the form of **JSON-like documents** (BSON), making it easy to represent hierarchical data structures.

   o MongoDB is highly **scalable** and is often used for web applications that need flexibility in how data is stored and queried.

   Example of a MongoDB query (using MongoDB's shell or a driver):

   javascript

   ```javascript
   db.users.find({ "username": "johndoe" });
   ```

Integrating Databases into Your Web Application

To integrate a database into your web application, you typically need to:

1. **Install the database driver or ORM** for the database you plan to use. For example:

   o For **MySQL** or **PostgreSQL**, you can use mysql2 or pg for Node.js.

- For **MongoDB**, you can use mongoose, a popular ODM (Object Data Modeling) library for MongoDB.

2. **Set up a database connection** in your application. This involves configuring the database connection string and establishing a connection to the database server.

Example for MongoDB using Mongoose:

javascript

```
const mongoose = require('mongoose');

mongoose.connect('mongodb://localhost:27017/mydb', {
  useNewUrlParser: true,
  useUnifiedTopology: true
})
.then(() => console.log('Connected to MongoDB'))
.catch(err => console.error('Could not connect to MongoDB:', err));
```

3. **Define models** for the data you wish to store and interact with. In MongoDB, for example, you define a schema using Mongoose.

Example of a Mongoose schema:

javascript

```
const mongoose = require('mongoose');

const userSchema = new mongoose.Schema({
```

```
username: { type: String, required: true },
email: { type: String, required: true },
password: { type: String, required: true }
});
```

```
const User = mongoose.model('User', userSchema);
```

4. **Perform CRUD operations** (Create, Read, Update, Delete) using the database.

Example for creating a new user with MongoDB (Mongoose):

javascript

```
const user = new User({
  username: 'johndoe',
  email: 'johndoe@example.com',
  password: 'hashedpassword123'
});
```

```
user.save()
  .then(() => console.log('User saved'))
  .catch(err => console.error('Error saving user:', err));
```

Real-World Example: Building a CRUD App with MongoDB and Express.js

Let's walk through creating a simple **CRUD app** with **MongoDB** and **Express.js**. In this app, we will create an API that allows us to manage **users** (create, read, update, and delete users).

Step 1: Set Up the Project

1. Create a new directory for the project and navigate into it:

    bash

    ```
    mkdir crud-app
    cd crud-app
    ```

2. Initialize the project and install dependencies:

    bash

    ```
    npm init -y
    npm install express mongoose body-parser
    ```

3. Create a new file called app.js and set up the basic server and MongoDB connection:

    javascript

    ```
    const express = require('express');
    const mongoose = require('mongoose');
    const bodyParser = require('body-parser');
    const app = express();
    ```

```
app.use(bodyParser.json());

// MongoDB connection
mongoose.connect('mongodb://localhost:27017/crudapp', {
  useNewUrlParser: true,
  useUnifiedTopology: true
})
.then(() => console.log('Connected to MongoDB'))
.catch(err => console.error('Could not connect to MongoDB:', err));

// Define User schema and model
const userSchema = new mongoose.Schema({
  username: String,
  email: String
});

const User = mongoose.model('User', userSchema);

// Create user
app.post('/users', (req, res) => {
  const user = new User(req.body);
  user.save()
    .then(user => res.status(201).json(user))
    .catch(err => res.status(400).json({ error: err.message }));
});

// Get all users
app.get('/users', (req, res) => {
  User.find()
    .then(users => res.json(users))
```

```
    .catch(err => res.status(400).json({ error: err.message }));
});

// Get user by ID
app.get('/users/:id', (req, res) => {
  const { id } = req.params;
  User.findById(id)
    .then(user => res.json(user))
    .catch(err => res.status(404).json({ error: 'User not found' }));
});

// Update user
app.put('/users/:id', (req, res) => {
  const { id } = req.params;
  User.findByIdAndUpdate(id, req.body, { new: true })
    .then(user => res.json(user))
    .catch(err => res.status(400).json({ error: err.message }));
});

// Delete user
app.delete('/users/:id', (req, res) => {
  const { id } = req.params;
  User.findByIdAndDelete(id)
    .then(() => res.status(204).send())
    .catch(err => res.status(400).json({ error: err.message }));
});

// Start the server
app.listen(3000, () => console.log('Server running on
http://localhost:3000'));
```

Step 2: Run the Server

Now, run the server:

bash

node app.js

The server will be running on http://localhost:3000. You can now test the **CRUD** operations:

- **POST** /users: Create a new user.
- **GET** /users: Get all users.
- **GET** /users/:id: Get a specific user by ID.
- **PUT** /users/:id: Update a user by ID.
- **DELETE** /users/:id: Delete a user by ID.

You can use **Postman** or **cURL** to test these API routes.

Summary

In this chapter, we explored the differences between **relational databases** (e.g., MySQL and PostgreSQL) and **NoSQL databases** (e.g., MongoDB), discussing the strengths and weaknesses of each type. We also learned how to integrate databases into web applications, focusing on setting up connections and performing CRUD operations.

Finally, we built a **real-world example** of a **CRUD application with MongoDB** and **Express.js**, demonstrating how to create, read, update, and delete user data. This example serves as a foundation for integrating **MongoDB** into your full-stack web applications and highlights the power and flexibility of NoSQL databases for handling large, dynamic datasets.

Chapter 23: Introduction to Web Security

Web security is a critical aspect of modern web development. With increasing cyber threats, it's essential to understand how to secure web applications effectively. This chapter will introduce you to **key security concepts** such as **HTTPS**, **CSRF**, and **XSS**, and will cover **best practices for securing web applications**. We'll also walk through a **real-world example** that demonstrates how to **implement password hashing** and **JWT security** to protect user data in a Node.js application.

Key Security Concepts for Web Applications

1. **HTTPS (HyperText Transfer Protocol Secure)**:
   - **HTTPS** is a protocol used to secure the communication between the client (browser) and the server. It encrypts the data exchanged using **SSL/TLS encryption**, which protects against eavesdropping, man-in-the-middle attacks, and tampering.
   - **Why is HTTPS important?**
     - Ensures the privacy and integrity of data transmitted between the client and server.

- Protects sensitive information like passwords, credit card details, and personal data from being intercepted.
- Google has made HTTPS a ranking factor, so securing your site can improve SEO.

How to use HTTPS:

- Obtain an **SSL certificate** from a trusted certificate authority (CA).
- Set up your server (e.g., using **Express** or **Apache**) to serve traffic over HTTPS.
- Redirect HTTP requests to HTTPS to ensure secure connections.

2. **CSRF (Cross-Site Request Forgery)**:
   - **CSRF** is a type of attack where a malicious user tricks the authenticated user into making unwanted requests to the web application. It exploits the trust that a site has in a user's browser.
   - **Example**: A logged-in user might unknowingly perform actions like transferring money or changing account settings if the attacker tricks them into clicking a malicious link.

How to prevent CSRF:

o Use **CSRF tokens**: Include a unique token in each form or request to ensure that the request originates from your website.

o Validate the origin of requests by checking the Origin or Referer headers.

3. **XSS (Cross-Site Scripting)**:

o **XSS** occurs when an attacker injects malicious scripts (usually JavaScript) into a web application. The script runs in the context of the user's browser, allowing attackers to steal cookies, session tokens, or execute malicious actions on behalf of the user.

o **Example**: An attacker could inject a script into a comment field that captures the user's session cookie and sends it to the attacker.

How to prevent XSS:

o **Sanitize inputs**: Always sanitize and escape user input to remove any malicious code.

o **Content Security Policy (CSP)**: Implement a CSP header to restrict which sources of JavaScript can be executed on your site.

o **Use HTTPS**: Since XSS exploits often involve injecting scripts over HTTP, using HTTPS can reduce the risk by ensuring secure transmission.

Best Practices for Securing Web Apps

1. **Use Strong Authentication**:
   - o **Password Hashing**: Never store passwords in plaintext. Use a strong hashing algorithm like **bcrypt** to hash passwords before storing them.
   - o **Multi-Factor Authentication (MFA)**: Add an extra layer of security by requiring users to authenticate with something they know (password) and something they have (e.g., OTP sent to their phone).

2. **Protect Sensitive Data**:
   - o **Encryption**: Encrypt sensitive data both in transit (using HTTPS) and at rest (in the database) to protect it from unauthorized access.
   - o **Use Environment Variables**: Store sensitive data like API keys, database credentials, and other secrets in environment variables, not in your codebase.

3. **Implement Proper Authorization**:
   - o Ensure that users can only access resources and perform actions they are authorized to do. Implement role-based access control (RBAC) or attribute-based access control (ABAC).
   - o **JWT (JSON Web Tokens)**: Use JWT for stateless user authentication. Ensure that tokens are signed

and optionally encrypted to protect against tampering.

4. **Prevent SQL Injection**:
   - Always use **parameterized queries** or **ORMs (Object-Relational Mappers)** to prevent SQL injection attacks.
   - Never concatenate user input directly into SQL queries. Always treat user input as untrusted.

5. **Regularly Update Dependencies**:
   - Ensure that your application and its dependencies are up to date to protect against known vulnerabilities.
   - Use tools like **npm audit** or **Snyk** to check for vulnerabilities in your dependencies.

6. **Security Headers**:
   - Use HTTP security headers like **X-Content-Type-Options**, **X-Frame-Options**, **Strict-Transport-Security**, and **Content-Security-Policy** to reduce the attack surface.

Real-World Example: Implementing Password Hashing and JWT Security

In this example, we will create a simple **user authentication system** using **JWT** and **bcrypt** for password hashing in **Node.js** and **Express**.

Step 1: Set Up the Project

1. Create a new project directory and initialize it:

   bash

   ```bash
   mkdir jwt-auth
   cd jwt-auth
   npm init -y
   npm install express jsonwebtoken bcryptjs body-parser
   ```

2. Create the app.js file and set up the Express server:

   javascript

   ```javascript
   const express = require('express');
   const bcrypt = require('bcryptjs');
   const jwt = require('jsonwebtoken');
   const bodyParser = require('body-parser');
   const app = express();
   const JWT_SECRET = 'your_jwt_secret'; // Use a stronger secret in production
   const users = []; // Dummy in-memory storage for demonstration

   app.use(bodyParser.json());

   // Register endpoint
   app.post('/register', async (req, res) => {
     const { username, password } = req.body;
   ```

```
// Check if user already exists
if (users.find(user => user.username === username)) {
  return res.status(400).send('User already exists');
}

// Hash the password before storing it
const hashedPassword = await bcrypt.hash(password, 10);
users.push({ username, password: hashedPassword });
res.status(201).send('User registered');
});

// Login endpoint
app.post('/login', async (req, res) => {
  const { username, password } = req.body;
  const user = users.find(user => user.username === username);

  if (!user) {
    return res.status(400).send('User not found');
  }

// Compare provided password with the stored hashed password
const isValidPassword = await bcrypt.compare(password, user.password);
  if (!isValidPassword) {
    return res.status(400).send('Invalid password');
  }

// Generate JWT token
const token = jwt.sign({ username: user.username }, JWT_SECRET, { expiresIn: '1h' });
```

```
      res.json({ token });
   });


   // Protected route
   app.get('/dashboard', (req, res) => {
     const token = req.header('Authorization')?.replace('Bearer ', '');

     if (!token) {
       return res.status(401).send('Access denied');
     }

     try {
       const decoded = jwt.verify(token, JWT_SECRET);
       res.json({ message: `Welcome, ${decoded.username}` });
     } catch (err) {
       res.status(400).send('Invalid token');
     }
   });


   app.listen(3000, () => console.log('Server running on
   http://localhost:3000'));
```

Step 2: Testing the Application

1. **Register a User**:
    o   Make a **POST** request to http://localhost:3000/register
        with the following body:

    json

    {

```
"username": "testuser",
"password": "password123"
}
```

2. **Login**:

   o   Make a **POST** request to http://localhost:3000/login with the same credentials.

   o   The response will contain a **JWT token**.

3. **Access Protected Route**:

   o   To access the **/dashboard** route, make a **GET** request to http://localhost:3000/dashboard and include the **JWT** in the Authorization header as a **Bearer token**:

makefile

```
Authorization: Bearer <your_jwt_token>
```

Summary

In this chapter, we covered essential **web security concepts** such as **HTTPS, CSRF**, and **XSS**. We also discussed **best practices for securing web applications**, including the use of **password hashing, JWT for authentication**, and **role-based authorization**.

We then implemented a **real-world example** of **password hashing with bcrypt** and **JWT security** in a Node.js application, demonstrating how to securely handle user login and protect routes in a web app. By following these security practices, you can help safeguard your web applications against common vulnerabilities and ensure that user data remains protected.

Chapter 24: Web Performance Optimization

Web performance is a crucial factor in the success of any modern web application. It directly impacts **user experience** (UX) and **SEO rankings**, which are essential for retaining visitors and improving site visibility. This chapter explores the **importance of web performance**, key **techniques for optimizing web performance**, and provides a **real-world example** of optimizing **image loading** in a **React app**.

Importance of Web Performance for User Experience and SEO

1. **User Experience (UX):**
   - **Fast loading times** are essential for a positive user experience. Slow websites can frustrate users, leading to higher bounce rates and lower engagement.
   - A slow site may also negatively impact user retention. Users are less likely to return to a website that consistently takes too long to load.
   - **Mobile users**, especially, expect quick responses due to varying network conditions. Therefore, performance optimization becomes even more critical in mobile-first environments.

2. **Search Engine Optimization (SEO)**:

   o **Google** and other search engines consider **page load speed** as a ranking factor. Slow sites are likely to rank lower in search results, reducing organic traffic.

   o Faster loading sites lead to better **user engagement metrics**, such as **time on site** and **lower bounce rates**, which in turn can positively influence SEO.

   o **Core Web Vitals**, introduced by Google, are a set of metrics focused on page speed and user interaction. Websites that score well in Core Web Vitals are more likely to rank higher in search engine results.

Key Takeaways:

- **Improved performance** results in a better user experience and better SEO rankings.
- Fast websites tend to keep visitors engaged and attract more organic traffic from search engines.

Techniques for Improving Web Performance

1. **Lazy Loading**:

   o **Lazy loading** is a technique that defers the loading of non-essential resources (like images or videos) until they are needed (e.g., when they come into the viewport as the user scrolls).

o   This reduces the initial loading time of the page by only loading critical resources on first request.

How Lazy Loading Improves Performance:

o   It decreases the time it takes for the page to load initially by avoiding loading large files right away.

o   It saves bandwidth for users, especially on mobile devices or slower networks, by only loading content that the user is about to see.

Example of Lazy Loading in React: React provides a built-in way to lazy load components using React.lazy() and Suspense:

javascript

```
import React, { Suspense, lazy } from 'react';

const LazyComponent = lazy(() => import('./LazyComponent'));

function App() {
 return (
  <div>
   <h1>Lazy Loaded Component</h1>
   <Suspense fallback={<div>Loading...</div>}>
    <LazyComponent />
   </Suspense>
```

```
    </div>
  );
}
```

export default App;

2. **Caching**:

    o **Caching** allows the browser or a CDN to store static resources, such as images, stylesheets, and scripts, so they don't need to be fetched every time a user visits a page.

    o There are several types of caching:

    - **Browser Cache**: Stores resources locally in the browser so they don't have to be downloaded again on subsequent visits.

    - **Server Cache**: Caches server-side responses to reduce the need for repeated database queries or computations.

    - **CDN Cache**: A Content Delivery Network (CDN) caches resources on servers distributed around the world, ensuring faster delivery to users based on their geographical location.

How Caching Improves Performance:

o Reduces the time spent fetching resources over the network.

o Minimizes server load by serving cached content rather than generating it dynamically.

Example of Cache-Control Headers: You can use Cache-Control headers to instruct the browser to cache certain assets:

http

Cache-Control: public, max-age=31536000

This tells the browser to cache the resource for one year.

3. **Minimizing HTTP Requests**:

o Every file loaded in a web page (HTML, CSS, JS, images) triggers an HTTP request. Reducing the number of HTTP requests can drastically improve page load times.

o Some ways to minimize HTTP requests:

▪ **Combine CSS and JS files**: Reduce the number of CSS and JavaScript files by combining them into a single file.

▪ **Image Sprites**: Combine multiple images into a single image and use CSS to display portions of it. This reduces the number of image requests.

- **Use Web Fonts efficiently**: Minimize the number of font files loaded.

How Reducing HTTP Requests Improves Performance:

o Fewer HTTP requests mean that the browser has to wait less time for each resource, resulting in faster page load times.

Real-World Example: Optimizing Image Loading in a React App
In this example, we'll demonstrate how to optimize image loading in a **React app** using **lazy loading** and **image compression**.

1. **Setting up Lazy Loading for Images**:
   o To implement **lazy loading** of images, we can use the loading="lazy" attribute in the img tag, which is supported natively by modern browsers.

Example:

jsx

```
import React from 'react';

const LazyImage = ({ src, alt }) => {
  return <img src={src} alt={alt} loading="lazy" />;
};
```

```
const App = () => {
  return (
   <div>
     <h1>Optimized Image Loading</h1>
     <LazyImage src="path/to/image1.jpg" alt="Image 1" />
     <LazyImage src="path/to/image2.jpg" alt="Image 2" />
     <LazyImage src="path/to/image3.jpg" alt="Image 3" />
   </div>
  );
};
```

export default App;

In the example above, the loading="lazy" attribute ensures that images are only loaded when they come into the viewport.

2. **Image Compression**:

   o Compressing images reduces their file size without sacrificing quality, improving load times.

   o You can use tools like **ImageOptim**, **TinyPNG**, or **webpack image-loader** to automatically compress images before serving them.

Example of Image Compression with Webpack:

   o Install the necessary loader:

   bash

npm install image-webpack-loader --save-dev

o **Configure it in** webpack.config.js:

javascript

```javascript
module.exports = {
  module: {
    rules: [
      {
        test: /\.(png|jpg|gif|svg)$/,
        use: [
          {
            loader: 'url-loader',
            options: {
              limit: 8192, // Inline images smaller than 8KB
              name: 'images/[name].[hash:8].[ext]',
            },
          },
          {
            loader: 'image-webpack-loader',
            options: {
              mozjpeg: {
                progressive: true,
                quality: 65,
              },
              optipng: {
                enabled: false,
              },
              pngquant: {
```

```
        quality: '65-90',
        speed: 4,
      },
      gifsicle: {
        interlaced: false,
      },
     },
    },
   ],
  },
 ],
},
};
```

This configuration compresses images as they are bundled by Webpack, reducing their size without compromising too much on quality.

3. **Responsive Images**:

   o   To ensure images are optimized for various screen sizes and resolutions, use the srcset attribute, which allows you to specify different image sizes based on the viewport width or device pixel ratio.

Example:

jsx

```
const ResponsiveImage = () => {
  return (
```

```
<img
  src="path/to/image.jpg"
  alt="Responsive Image"
  srcSet="path/to/image-320w.jpg   320w,   path/to/image-480w.jpg
480w, path/to/image-800w.jpg 800w"
  sizes="(max-width: 600px) 320px, (max-width: 1000px) 480px,
800px"
  />
);
};
```

In this example, the browser will choose the appropriate image size based on the device's screen width, improving performance on mobile devices and reducing unnecessary data usage.

Summary

In this chapter, we discussed the importance of **web performance** for both **user experience** and **SEO rankings**. We covered techniques such as **lazy loading, caching,** and **minimizing HTTP requests** to improve the performance of web applications.

We then provided a **real-world example** of **image loading optimization** in a **React app**, using techniques like **lazy loading, image compression,** and **responsive images** to ensure fast and efficient loading of images.

By implementing these techniques, you can significantly improve the performance of your web applications, leading to a better user experience, faster load times, and higher search engine rankings.

Chapter 25: Deploying and Maintaining Web Applications

Once your web application is built and tested, it's time to deploy it to a server so users can access it. Deployment and maintenance are crucial stages in the software development lifecycle, ensuring that the application is accessible, performs well, and is continuously updated. In this chapter, we'll cover the basics of **web hosting**, **domains**, and **DNS**, how to deploy applications to popular cloud platforms such as **AWS, Heroku**, and **DigitalOcean**, and how to set up **Continuous Integration/Continuous Deployment (CI/CD)**. We'll conclude with a **real-world example** of **deploying a Node.js app to Heroku**.

Introduction to Web Hosting, Domains, and DNS

1. **Web Hosting**:
   - **Web hosting** refers to the service that stores your web application and makes it accessible over the internet. Hosting providers offer a variety of services, from basic shared hosting to cloud infrastructure and specialized services for web apps.
   - The type of hosting you choose depends on your needs:

- **Shared Hosting**: Cost-effective but not very scalable, typically for simple websites.
- **VPS (Virtual Private Server)**: Offers more control and resources compared to shared hosting.
- **Cloud Hosting**: Scalable and flexible, suitable for growing applications.
- **Dedicated Hosting**: You have exclusive use of the server, ideal for high-traffic websites.

Popular web hosting providers include **Amazon Web Services (AWS)**, **Google Cloud Platform (GCP)**, **Microsoft Azure**, **DigitalOcean**, and **Heroku**.

2. **Domains**:
   - A **domain name** is the human-readable address of your website (e.g., example.com). It is used to map to an IP address where your application is hosted.
   - To get a domain, you must purchase it from a **domain registrar** such as **GoDaddy**, **Namecheap**, or **Google Domains**.
   - Once purchased, you need to link the domain to your hosting server through **DNS (Domain Name System)** settings.

3. **DNS (Domain Name System)**:

o **DNS** is like the phonebook of the internet. When you type a domain name in the browser, DNS translates it into an IP address to route the request to the correct server.

o When setting up a web application, you need to configure your DNS to point the domain to the server where your app is hosted. For example, after purchasing a domain from a registrar, you need to set up the **A record** or **CNAME record** to link your domain to your hosting provider.

Deploying Web Applications to Cloud Platforms

1. **Amazon Web Services (AWS)**:

   o AWS provides a wide range of cloud computing services, including **EC2** (Elastic Compute Cloud) for hosting virtual servers, **S3** (Simple Storage Service) for file storage, and **RDS** (Relational Database Service) for database management.

   o To deploy a web app on AWS, you typically:

   - Launch an EC2 instance.
   - Set up your server environment (e.g., install Node.js, Nginx).

- Deploy your application to the server using **SSH** or a deployment tool like **AWS Elastic Beanstalk**.
- Set up a **Route 53** DNS configuration to point your domain to the AWS instance.

2. **Heroku**:

   o **Heroku** is a **Platform as a Service (PaaS)** that abstracts away much of the complexity of deploying web applications. It allows you to deploy apps quickly using Git.

   o To deploy an application to Heroku:

      - Create a Heroku account and install the **Heroku CLI**.
      - Initialize a Git repository for your app if you haven't already.
      - Run commands to create a Heroku app and push your code to Heroku's cloud platform.
      - Heroku automatically handles scaling, monitoring, and updates.

   Heroku is an excellent choice for developers who want to focus on application development without managing servers.

3. **DigitalOcean**:

   o **DigitalOcean** is a cloud provider known for simplicity and cost-effective cloud infrastructure.

You can deploy web applications using **Droplets** (virtual private servers) or use their **App Platform** for automatic deployment and scaling.

- For traditional web application deployment, you would:
    - Create a Droplet (Linux-based server).
    - Install necessary software (e.g., Node.js, Nginx, database).
    - Deploy your app using **SSH** or **Git**.
    - Set up a domain with **DigitalOcean's DNS service** or link your custom domain.

Setting Up Continuous Integration/Continuous Deployment (CI/CD)

1. **What is CI/CD?**

    - **Continuous Integration (CI)** is the practice of automatically integrating code changes into a shared repository, running tests, and ensuring that the new code doesn't break the application.

    - **Continuous Deployment (CD)** automates the process of deploying the application to production whenever there is a change in the codebase.

2. **Why CI/CD?**

- o CI/CD improves development workflows by automating repetitive tasks, reducing errors, and ensuring that new features or bug fixes are deployed faster.
- o CI/CD tools such as **GitHub Actions**, **Jenkins**, and **CircleCI** can automate testing, deployment, and scaling of your application.

3. **Setting Up CI/CD**:
   - o To set up CI/CD for a Node.js application, you would typically:
     - Write tests for your application using tools like **Mocha**, **Jest**, or **Jasmine**.
     - Configure a CI tool to run tests automatically every time code is pushed to a repository.
     - Configure a CD pipeline to deploy the application to a server or cloud platform after successful tests.

Real-World Example: Deploying a Node.js App to Heroku

Let's walk through deploying a simple **Node.js application** to **Heroku**.

Step 1: Set Up the Node.js Application

1. Create a simple app.js file:

javascript

```javascript
const express = require('express');
const app = express();
const port = process.env.PORT || 3000;

app.get('/', (req, res) => {
  res.send('Hello, World!');
});

app.listen(port, () => {
  console.log(`App running on port ${port}`);
});
```

2. Create a package.json file (if not already created):

bash

```bash
npm init -y
npm install express
```

3. Test the app locally by running:

bash

```bash
node app.js
```

Step 2: Create a Heroku Account and Install the Heroku CLI

1. Go to Heroku and sign up for an account if you don't have
   one.

2. Install the **Heroku CLI** by following the instructions on the Heroku Dev Center.

Step 3: Deploy the App to Heroku

1. **Login to Heroku**:

   bash

   heroku login

2. **Initialize a Git repository** (if you haven't already):

   bash

   git init
   git add .
   git commit -m "Initial commit"

3. **Create a Heroku app**:

   bash

   heroku create

4. **Push your code to Heroku**:

   bash

   git push heroku master

5. **Access the app**: After the deployment completes, Heroku will provide a URL for your app (e.g., https://your-app-name.herokuapp.com). You can access your app through this URL.

Step 4: Set Up a Custom Domain (Optional)

1. You can add a custom domain to your Heroku app by going to your app's dashboard in the Heroku dashboard and adding your domain under the **Settings** tab.
2. Configure your domain's DNS to point to the Heroku app using the provided DNS target.

Summary

In this chapter, we covered essential concepts related to **deploying and maintaining web applications**. We discussed **web hosting**, **domains**, and **DNS**, and explored how to deploy applications to popular platforms like **AWS, Heroku**, and **DigitalOcean**.

We also looked at **Continuous Integration/Continuous Deployment (CI/CD)** and why automating your build and deployment process is essential for improving workflow efficiency.

Finally, we walked through the **real-world example** of deploying a **Node.js app to Heroku**, demonstrating how to push your code, access the application via a URL, and even configure a custom domain.

By mastering deployment and CI/CD, you can ensure that your web applications are easy to maintain, update, and scale, leading to a smoother experience for both developers and users.

Chapter 26: The Future of Web Development Frameworks

The web development landscape is continuously evolving, with new technologies and frameworks emerging to improve the development process, enhance user experiences, and address modern challenges. This chapter explores **emerging trends** in web development, including **JAMstack, WebAssembly**, and **serverless architectures**, discusses the **role of progressive web apps (PWAs)**, and highlights the **opportunities for developers** in the future of web technologies. We'll also provide a **real-world example** of **building a progressive web app (PWA)** with **React** and **Firebase**.

Emerging Trends in Web Development

1. **JAMstack (JavaScript, APIs, and Markup)**:
   - **JAMstack** is an architectural approach focused on improving the performance, scalability, and security of websites by decoupling the front-end from the back-end. It involves pre-rendering static pages and serving them from a CDN (Content Delivery Network), while dynamic interactions are powered by APIs.
   - **Key features**:

- **Static site generation**: Websites are pre-rendered into static files (HTML, CSS, and JavaScript) that are delivered quickly and securely.

- **Decoupling**: The front-end is separated from the back-end, allowing for easier updates and scaling.

- **APIs**: Server-side functionality is powered by APIs that are called when needed, allowing for dynamic content and real-time data.

o **Benefits of JAMstack**:

- **Speed**: Pre-rendered static pages load faster, improving performance and user experience.

- **Security**: Static sites are more secure since there's no server-side code running, reducing the attack surface.

- **Scalability**: By serving content via a CDN, JAMstack sites can handle large amounts of traffic easily.

Popular tools and frameworks for JAMstack development include **Next.js**, **Gatsby**, and **Hugo**.

2. **WebAssembly (Wasm)**:

- o **WebAssembly (Wasm)** is a binary instruction format that enables code written in any language (C, C++, Rust, etc.) to be compiled and run in the web browser at near-native speed.
- o **Why WebAssembly matters**:
  - **Performance**: Wasm allows web applications to run at speeds comparable to native applications, enabling more complex and computationally intensive tasks in the browser (e.g., video editing, 3D rendering).
  - **Language support**: WebAssembly allows developers to write code in languages other than JavaScript, broadening the possibilities for web development.
  - **Cross-platform**: Wasm runs on all major browsers, providing a cross-platform solution for web applications.

Examples of WebAssembly use cases:

- o Running **games** and **graphics rendering** in the browser.
- o **Scientific computing** and **machine learning** applications.
- o **Video editing** and other resource-intensive applications.

3. **Serverless Architectures**:
   - o **Serverless** is an architecture where developers can build and deploy applications without managing servers. In this model, cloud service providers automatically handle infrastructure provisioning, scaling, and maintenance.
   - o **How serverless works**:
     - Developers write code (functions) that is triggered by events (e.g., HTTP requests, database updates).
     - The cloud provider handles running the function, scaling it based on demand, and managing the underlying infrastructure.
   - o **Benefits of serverless**:
     - **Cost efficiency**: You only pay for the execution time of your code, reducing costs compared to maintaining always-on servers.
     - **Scalability**: The cloud provider automatically scales the functions based on demand, allowing for more efficient use of resources.
     - **Focus on business logic**: Developers can focus on writing the code and functionality without worrying about infrastructure management.

Popular serverless platforms include **AWS Lambda**, **Google Cloud Functions**, and **Azure Functions**.

The Role of Progressive Web Apps (PWAs) in Modern Web Development

Progressive Web Apps (PWAs) are web applications that use modern web technologies to deliver an app-like experience on the web. PWAs can be installed on a user's device, work offline, and offer push notifications, combining the best features of both web and mobile apps.

1. **Key features of PWAs**:
   - **Offline functionality**: PWAs can work offline or with a poor network connection by caching resources and data locally on the user's device.
   - **App-like experience**: PWAs provide a smooth, native app-like experience, including fast loading times and responsiveness.
   - **Push notifications**: PWAs can send push notifications to users, helping with engagement and retention.
   - **Installation**: Users can install PWAs on their home screens, just like native apps, without needing to go through an app store.

2. **Why PWAs are important**:

   o **Improved user engagement**: The ability to send push notifications and work offline increases user retention and engagement.

   o **Cross-platform**: PWAs can run on any device with a browser, reducing the need for separate web and mobile apps.

   o **Cost-effective**: Since PWAs don't require separate mobile app development, they save time and resources compared to building native apps.

Opportunities for Developers in the Future of Web Technologies

As web technologies continue to evolve, there are several exciting opportunities for developers:

1. **Specializing in JAMstack**: As more companies adopt JAMstack architecture for better performance, scalability, and security, developers who specialize in JAMstack technologies (e.g., static site generators, APIs, and CDNs) will be in high demand.

2. **Working with WebAssembly**: With the performance improvements offered by WebAssembly, developers who can write in languages like **Rust** and **C++** and compile to

Wasm will have an edge in areas like gaming, scientific computing, and high-performance applications on the web.

3. **Serverless Development**: The increasing adoption of serverless architectures means developers with expertise in **AWS Lambda, Google Cloud Functions**, or **Azure Functions** will be sought after, especially for building scalable applications with minimal infrastructure management.

4. **PWAs and Mobile Development**: With the rise of PWAs, developers who can build mobile-first web apps with offline capabilities and push notifications will find themselves in demand for delivering rich, app-like experiences on the web.

Real-World Example: Building a Progressive Web App with React and Firebase

Let's walk through creating a simple **Progressive Web App (PWA)** using **React** and **Firebase**.

Step 1: Set Up the React Application

1. Create a new React app:

bash

```
npx create-react-app pwa-example
cd pwa-example
```

2. Install the necessary dependencies:

bash

npm install firebase

Step 2: Setting Up Firebase for Push Notifications and Hosting

1. Go to Firebase Console, create a new project, and enable **Firebase Cloud Messaging (FCM)** for push notifications.
2. In the Firebase console, get the Firebase config for your app, which includes keys like apiKey, authDomain, etc.
3. Initialize Firebase in your React app by adding the Firebase config in src/firebase.js:

javascript

```javascript
import firebase from 'firebase/app';
import 'firebase/messaging';

const firebaseConfig = {
  apiKey: 'YOUR_API_KEY',
  authDomain: 'YOUR_AUTH_DOMAIN',
  projectId: 'YOUR_PROJECT_ID',
  messagingSenderId: 'YOUR_SENDER_ID',
  appId: 'YOUR_APP_ID',
};

// Initialize Firebase
firebase.initializeApp(firebaseConfig);
```

```javascript
const messaging = firebase.messaging();
```

```javascript
export { messaging };
```

Step 3: Add Service Worker for Offline Support

1. In public/, modify service-worker.js to enable caching and offline support.
2. Register the service worker in src/index.js:

javascript

```javascript
import * as serviceWorkerRegistration from './serviceWorkerRegistration';
```

```javascript
serviceWorkerRegistration.register();
```

Step 4: Implement Push Notifications

1. In src/App.js, add code to request permission for push notifications:

javascript

```javascript
import React, { useEffect } from 'react';
import { messaging } from './firebase';

const App = () => {
  useEffect(() => {
    messaging
      .requestPermission()
```

```
    .then(() => messaging.getToken())
    .then(token => console.log('FCM Token:', token))
    .catch(err => console.error('Error getting FCM token:', err));
}, []);

return <div className="App">Hello, World!</div>;
};

export default App;
```

Step 5: Deploy to Firebase Hosting

1. Install Firebase CLI:

bash

```
npm install -g firebase-tools
```

2. Initialize Firebase Hosting:

bash

```
firebase init
```

3. Build the React app and deploy it:

bash

```
npm run build
firebase deploy
```

Your PWA is now live, and users can install it on their devices and receive push notifications, all with offline functionality.

CONCLUSION

In this chapter, we discussed **emerging trends** in web development, such as **JAMstack**, **WebAssembly**, and **serverless architectures**. We also explored the significance of **Progressive Web Apps (PWAs)** and how they provide an app-like experience in the browser, improving user engagement and performance. We then walked through a **real-world example** of building a **PWA with React** and **Firebase**, covering everything from offline support to push notifications and deployment.

The future of web development offers exciting opportunities, particularly for developers who specialize in new technologies like **WebAssembly**, **JAMstack**, and **serverless architectures**. Embracing these innovations will help developers build faster, more scalable, and engaging web applications.

www.ingramcontent.com/pod-product-compliance
Lightning Source LLC
LaVergne TN
LVHW051433050326
832903LV00030BD/3069

* 9 7 9 8 3 0 7 8 1 4 8 9 5 *